EX LIBRIS

The Knitting Sutra

ALSO BY SUSAN GORDON LYDON

Take the Long Way Home

3/12/97

To Leigh,

The Knitting Sutra

CRAFT AS A SPIRITUAL PRACTICE

Susan Gordon Lydon

with best wishes

Susan Gordon Lydon

HarperSanFrancisco
An Imprint of HarperCollins*Publishers*

THE KNITTING SUTRA: *Craft as a Spiritual Practice.* Copyright © 1997 by Susan Gordon Lydon. All rights reserved. Printed in the United States of America. No part of this book may be used or reproduced in any manner whatsoever without written permission except in the case of brief quotations embodied in critical articles and reviews. For information address HarperCollins Publishers, 10 East 53rd Street, New York, NY 10022.

HarperCollins Web Site: http://www.harpercollins.com
HarperCollins®, 📖 ®, and HarperSanFrancisco™ are trademarks of HarperCollins Publishers Inc.

FIRST EDITION

Library of Congress Cataloging-in-Publication Data
Lydon, Susan Gordon.
The knitting Sutra : craft as a spiritual practice / Susan Gordon Lydon — 1st ed.
ISBN 0–06–251202–1 (cloth)
ISBN 0–06–251203–X (pbk.)
1. Knitting — Philosophy. 2. Spirituality. I. Title.
TT820.L93   1997   746.43'2'01 — dc20   96–34368

97 98 99 00 01 ❖ RRDH 10 9 8 7 6 5 4 3 2

For Lorraine, Sheila, Ricky, Debbie,
and all the women who knit too much

CONTENTS

Introduction: The View from the Factory   1

1. A Broken Wing   13

2. Knitting the Bone   19

3. Transfiguration of the Blues   27

4. A Life Made by Hand   41

5. Spider Woman's Daughters   53

6. Winged Hearts   67

7. Desperately Seeking   77

8. Earth Walk   89

9. God and Nature, Nature and Cloth   95

10. Dreaming of Dragons   111

11. A Secret Weapon   123

12. The Knitting Sutra   135

13. The Zen of Nonattachment   145

Epilogue: Taking Flight   155

Acknowledgments   159

The lyf so short, the crafte so long to lerne.

Geoffrey Chaucer

Introduction:
The View from the Factory

LOU, MY CLOSEST FRIEND, comes over to visit, but there's nowhere for her to sit. Every available chair is taken up with pieces of knitting in varying stages of completion. I am doing what I call production knitting, working on five or so projects all at the same time. It's a laugh, really, my ability to produce. This work is extremely labor intensive; it takes so much time for me to finish the same garment a machine could spit out in minutes that it's ludicrous to think of what I do, my feeble two-handed activity, as "production."

Never mind, though, because I'm knitting every moment of the day, throwing off by-products like a smelter. The intensity of my knitting matches the intensity of my writing. There's some kind of symbiosis here, though I'd be hard-pressed to explain just how it works. During a time of feverish activity composing first-draft material for a book, I'm also producing: songs, poems, articles, and sweaters, plus a journal I've named "The Zombie Chronicles," whose contents should be obvious from its title. My creativity is gushing like a river at flood tide, and I can't really direct its flow. My mind works so fast I can't keep up; that's why I have to start so many projects and then race around trying to make progress on all of them at once.

Master knitter or demon knitter? You be the judge.

I'm also an impatient knitter, which should be an oxymoron but in my case isn't. I embark on a project involving hundreds of thousands of stitches, and then I'm in a hurry to get them all done. My impatience is the reason I hate to rip out. It also makes me want to begin knitting the moment I bring my yarn home from the store. These days I force myself to make swatches for gauge, but believe me, it wasn't always so. And why should such an impatient person be knitting in the first place? Why not race cars? Or bake cookies? Do something you actually can finish in twenty minutes? As the Yiddish expression goes, *nicht bashert*: it wasn't meant to be.

So I'm forced to suspend time. To work outside of time. To forget that time exists. On a subconscious level I have to believe that I have all the time in the world, or I wouldn't be able to begin. And something happens when I entertain that fallacy. Time, which is fractal, stretches out, and I begin to experience eternity. There is something about that spacious expansion into endless time that promotes the growth of large-scale thinking, that enables one to rise above the petty stresses of everyday life. Viewed from a certain perspective, time is the only real luxury we have.

Sylvia Boorstein, a Vipassana Buddhist meditation teacher, used to teach a course at the Spirit Rock Meditation Center in northern California called "Hand Needlework as Concentration Practice." As she describes it, during the first hour everyone did needlework—knitting, crocheting, embroidery, needlepoint—in silence. During the second hour, all continued to do needlework while speaking deeply to the others about their lives, sharing "out of the space of composure" and listening "out of a space of balance. Everyone agreed that the hour of concentration practice was what allowed us to share so deeply," she continues in her book *It's Easier Than You*

Think. "Concentration practice strengthens *and* softens the mind. That's not a paradox. It's true."

☙

Handcrafts belong to an earlier world, the slower pace of preindustrial life where one had the leisure to sink deeply and profoundly into the rhythms of nature within and without and to feel a connection with the earth as a living spiritual entity. We make things by hand to express who we are, our identity as individuals as well as our affiliation to our tribe or our clan. Handcrafts throughout history have often been fashioned with the aid of prayer, one prayer for each bead or each stitch, while keeping good thoughts to enhance the spiritual purpose of the object. It is no accident that some of the finest lace in Europe was fashioned in convents; like the counting of the rosary, the motions of needlework are singularly well suited to the practice of contemplation.

Self-expression, whether individual or tribal, religious or secular, is to my mind one of the most beautiful impulses that we humans possess. We look at our brief time here on earth; we perceive our inconsequentiality in a vast universe of planets and stars; we know our connectedness to our ancestors and descendants and feel our mortality as we pass along the eternal continuum of time; and yet we still want others to know who we were, how we lived, that we were here and saw and felt and knew beauty. The pioneer women with lives of endless work, half buried underground in sod houses on the prairies, often without trees or neighbors for company, fashioned quilts out of pieces of cloth, which might have been the only color they saw for months on end. The creation of those quilts was, as many have appreciated since, a monumental work.

I myself have spent many hours in the company of those women. First, in the years when I began collecting patchwork quilts. Later, when I began piecing fabric together myself. And now, when, with each piece of handwork I do, I connect with the centuries of women who cultivated their inner lives and expressed them through the humble works of their hands. The making of crafts can be, at the same time, both solitary and communal in equal measure. Old-time quilting bees often provided groups of women with rare opportunities for social life, and, in the same way, women often knit together companionably so that the work they do becomes at once individual and collective. Memoirs of Native American family life often mention scenes of women sitting around a kitchen table bent over their beadwork, talking softly among themselves. These scenes remind me of my childhood, when I always wanted to stay in the kitchen with the older female relatives as they worked and gossiped together.

In my frenzies of production knitting, I also feel a kinship with the women of the British Isles who knitted constantly to keep their families supplied with food and necessities. I once heard Alice Starmore, the doyenne of Fair Isle knitting, a style of multicolored patterning much prized throughout the world, state in a lecture that a Fair Isle woman had to produce one complete sweater a week to put food on her table. I find that almost impossible to believe, the sweaters are of such a complexity and difficulty. Commercial Fair Isle sweaters were knitted small and then stretched wet on wooden forms to make the most of the precious yarns provided by merchants, so that the knitters' families might cadge some leftover yarn for their own needs.

I have also read accounts of whole families constructing "fisher gansies," sweaters fishermen wore to sea. Younger daughters were assigned to the ribbing and the plain parts and older sisters to the patterned stitches, while Mum wove the shoulders and grafted the neck.

Though knitting is a consistent feature in many northern countries with chilly climates, it found some of its highest expression in the remote isles around Scotland, including the Outer Hebrides, Alice Starmore's home.

From there it was exported to other parts of the world. Scottish missionaries, for example, taught knitting to the Salish Indians of Canada, whose local artisans transformed it into an indigenous art form still practiced today. The Cowichan sweaters, as they're called, are made of strong yarn spun to the thickness of a finger, then knitted into rugged, waterproof jackets with geometric patterns and nature motifs. The designer Ralph Lauren once included some Cowichan sweaters in one of his collections. While the local knitters were pleased to have their work shown to such advantage in the outside world, Lauren was in for a shock when he tried to take credit for the designs they had knitted. The knitters knew not only where each design came from and how long it had been in use, but also who had invented it in the first place.

Handknitting is a luxury rather than a necessity for me, though I sometimes sell what I've made when I need the money. On the whole I knit because I love to knit, because the process of designing and then fashioning a piece of clothing with my hands is something that has excited and inspired me since childhood. In my generation we've all heard the famous dictum of Joseph Campbell, the historian of mythology: "Follow your bliss, and doors will open where there are no doors." If I were to truly

follow my bliss, I'd probably be sewing, knitting, or beading every minute of the day, making one-of-a-kind garments and pouches and whatnots, expecting money to
fall from the sky so that I could afford my materials and
pay my bills. We knitters have a secret passion: to clothe
ourselves and our families and friends (and occasionally
perfect strangers) in marvelous colors and textures and
warmth.

The process of inventing the project and assembling
the materials and starting the manufacture is, of course,
far more thrilling than the patient working through to
the end, the 90 percent of the work that takes place after
the original inspiration is gone. In the knitting factory I
try to keep a balance of simple and complicated, new
and almost-finished, things for others and things for myself. I try to have enough variety so that when I get bored
with one thing, I can pick up another; some of my projects are portable and can be done with company; some
can only be done at home alone, with total concentration and no distractions.

And no matter how many I have going at once, I always crave another one.

I should be home writing, working toward a deadline;
instead I'm at the Knitting Basket, my favorite local yarn
store, poring over yarns, leafing through patterns, chat-

ting with Linda, who owns the shop, about the events of both our lives.

"How's the writing going?" she asks me as I walk in the door.

"Not as well as the knitting," I answer. "Tell me, Linda, how come I have five projects going and I'm coming in here to buy yarn for a new one? Am I crazy, or what?"

"Let's face it," she says with a shrug of her shoulders, "we're all junkies."

Everyone in the store laughs. We all share a common vice. The appeal may be hard to see if you're looking at it only from outside, but experience it yourself and you may find it more attractive than you ever thought possible.

Knitters enjoy a strange obsession. Possibly, our enthusiasm can be communicated only from one to another. I have found on the Internet that knitters are so overly fond of sharing their joy that one subscribes to a knitting list at one's peril. The volume of messages generated by the community of knitters on the Internet is nothing short of astonishing, especially considering the juxtaposition of such an ancient form of craft with such a modern form of technology. But knitters have another surprising quality: our aptitude for mathematics, displayed only offhandedly, of course, in writing patterns or figuring out how to translate instructions from one gauge and size to another.

Knitting is taught to all grades in Rudolf Steiner's Waldorf Schools because, along with improving hand-eye coordination, it helps the children feel comfortable with numbers.

⚮

Two things have occurred to me over and over again while knitting. One is the old saw about the devil making work for idle hands, except with a twist. If the devil makes work for idle hands, then could constantly busy hands entice angels to whisper in the knitter's ear? And is it possible that female spirituality through the ages may have been concealed in the minutiae of domestic life rather than expressed in the grandiosity and pomposity of churches and sermons?

Women experience so many pressures to give up being who they truly are in order to take care of everyone around them. And yet I have seen women flower creatively only when they finally learn how to ruthlessly protect their time. This is, however, a comparative luxury of the present. And it also comes with a disadvantage. Television has made an enemy of silence so that silence today is suspect, a stranger in most American homes. But silence, like the interior world, is by its very nature vast and limitless, with infinite rather than finite possibilities.

It nourishes like food for the soul; it is the space where prayer, meditation, and inspiration flourish. Silence, as the old expression goes, is golden. Only in silence can you hear the voice of God.

I have learned those lessons for myself only now in my middle years. I know I have to guard my time and privacy, or I won't have the space to write and think. I have deliberately cultivated solitude and the ability to live in silence. And I have found knitting to be an aid in all those things. After all, the important thing is not so much what you knit as what happens to you while you knit it. Where the interior journey takes you. What you find there. How you are transformed when you come back home.

This is a book about a journey into spirituality through the medium of craft. It involves the finding of a treasure that was nearly lost to me and the pursuit of that treasure with the renewed passion of reunion. Though I've been knitting all my adult life, it took the shock of an accident and its attendant change of perspective to make me appreciate the value of the craft and delve deeply into its mysteries, following where it led.

What I found is that this tiny domestic world of knitting is endless; it runs broader and deeper than anyone might imagine. It is infinite and seemingly inexhaustible in its capacity to inspire, excite, and provoke creative insight.

The activity itself is satisfying, addictive, absorbing, enjoyable, and productive. It is soothing and meditative in nature. And as an added bonus, it results in something useful in the end.

That's why there's no place for Lou to sit down in my house. Lou may be my best friend, but knitting is my life.

CHAPTER ONE

A Broken Wing

I USED TO LAUGH when my daughter described me as "my mother, with both feet firmly planted in midair." But that was before I actually landed there, stepping backward off a deck literally into thin air.

I was visiting some friends in the Napa Valley who've built two houses on a mountainside there. The late summer day was hot and lazy, and I sat on the upper deck watching hummingbirds come to a feeder. I wanted to study the birds in more detail, so I began to back away from them, trying to fix them in focus in my binoculars.

There's nothing more shocking, in my experience, than bringing your foot down, expecting solid ground, and finding, after it's too late and you've already lost your balance, that you're stepping into empty space. I tumbled off the deck, arms flung back, binoculars flying, before I even knew what had happened.

I don't recall touching down; I must have blacked out as I landed. When I again became conscious, I was rolling and bumping down a flight of wooden stairs. Time had slowed, the way it does when your life is threatened. I felt as though I had been and would continue to be falling down those stairs forever, like Alice down the rabbit hole. "Everything will be different now," I thought to myself. Somewhere in the far reaches of my mind loomed a clear understanding of how, in a single second, one tiny misstep could suddenly change a person's life.

I finally came to rest at the foot of the garden stairs, legs splayed out in a strawberry patch, upper body flung across the bottom step. My right arm hurt, with a burning sensation, somewhere between my shoulder and elbow.

As it would later turn out, a doctor friend we called from the house diagnosed my problem without even seeing me. "It sounds like a broken humerus," he said. "They won't be able to put it in a cast, because if they did you'd never be able to move your shoulder again. They'll probably give you a sling."

Soon a fire truck, ambulance, and what seemed at the time like a car full of local politicians appeared on the scene, sirens blaring. I thought the paramedics would give me something for the pain, which by now was intense and throbbing, but they had to see if I'd suffered a head injury first, so they put me on a stretcher and began the long trek to the hospital. The dirt road down the mountain was rutted and bumpy; each time the ambulance jolted and jostled my arm, I sobbed with pain. I asked the paramedic what he thought had happened, if I had torn a muscle or a tendon. I worried that my injury wouldn't be severe enough to justify this degree of drama, more fearful of embarrassment than I was of being disabled. I felt guilty about having ruined everyone's weekend.

My hostess sat with me at Queen of the Valley Hospital; it took hours before anyone in the emergency room got around to seeing me.

Finally, after a painful series of X rays, a nurse appeared at my bedside with a syringe in her hand. "You've got a really nasty break there," she said. "No wonder you're in so much pain."

I'd been in recovery from opiate addiction for almost five years, without so much as a pain pill in that time, and the shot of Demerol the nurse gave me felt so strong I thought I would leave my body. It occurred to me that I should ask for something nonnarcotic, but I was just in too much pain to refuse the relief, so long in coming, that now crept over my ravaged body.

∽

It seems a truism, but until it happens to you it's almost impossible to understand how helpless you can be with one of your hands or arms out of commission. The simplest tasks presented a complex engineering challenge to me; I couldn't drive, write, or cook, and it sometimes took me all day just to accomplish the barest minimum of life-sustaining activities. My friends did my grocery shopping and drove me to my various medical appointments: orthopedic specialist, chiropractor, Chinese herbalist. I liked to call the crowded orthopedist's office the "Boulevard of Broken Bones."

Others made jokes as well. "Bird-watching. Not for the faint of heart," said one of my daughter's friends when I told him what had happened. "Next time why don't you try bungee jumping instead?" My friend Peter Mitchell claimed I had fallen because "not being from California, you don't have 'deck sense.' If it had been a fire escape you would have been fine."

Of course the truth was far more mysterious and, as usual, remained inscrutable. Looking back it seems as though the hummingbird I'd been watching led me off the deck and into an unknown world so I could learn something that wouldn't have been accessible to me unless I shed everything familiar and approached my life from a different perspective.

I've always been the kind of person who worked with my hands. I sewed, knitted, beaded, did needlepoint and embroidery, crocheted, and drew. I've worked out many problems in my mind while my sewing machine needle flew across the fabric or my hands performed some rhythmic repetitive task. None of these things did I take all that seriously. If anyone had asked me, I would have described them as hobbies, though frequently I earned money from them. But the thought of losing the ability to do them was almost beyond my power to comprehend and forced me to view them in a whole new light.

The fall had shaken loose my other preconceptions as well, particularly about spirituality. I believe now that I was in some sort of spiritual crisis at the time. As the Navajo medicine man I eventually consulted told me, I had fallen out of harmony with the natural world. I felt fragmented and uncentered, shaky at the core; the beliefs and practices that had nourished my spirit in previous years no longer seemed to be working, and I had begun casting about for something new, I didn't know what.

Sometimes a fall shakes everything up, and the pieces configure in a new way. Unbeknownst to me, I was about to embark on a series of inward and outward journeys that would drop me off in a different place from where I had started. They were adventures I probably would have avoided had I not broken my right arm. In retrospect, it was the perfect calamity-as-opportunity scenario, in more ways than one, but of course this would only become clear over time.

In the right brain/left brain theory of how the human mind works, the left lobe of the cerebral cortex, which produces thought that is analytical and ordered, more mathematical in nature, goes with the right hand, while the right lobe—poetic, musical, intuitive, and creative— is associated with the workings of the left hand. At the time I broke my arm I was struggling with the rewrite of a book. My editor had told me I was mired in chronology, trapped in linear thinking. He wanted my work to be organized more imaginatively. Now, like it or not, I would be forced to rely on my left hand—and the right side of my brain—to learn this lesson the hard way. That seemed as plausible an explanation as any for what had happened.

Everyone I knew had something to say about my so-called accident. But it was my daughter, who knows me better than anyone else, who came up with the theory closest to home. "Well, Mom," she asked, "were you try-ing to see if you could fly?"

CHAPTER TWO

Knitting the Bone

WITH MY RIGHT ARM IN A SLING, it was virtually impossible to accomplish the tasks I normally took for granted, but that was not my worst problem. Pain consumed my mind and drove away thoughts of anything inessential. Intense physical pain makes you realize what a luxury it is to feel emotional pain, though that can often seem more distressing. But physical pain inhabits you in every corner of your being, so that you become pain itself and lose your normal identity.

I struggled to deal with daily life, kept my schedule of medical appointments, and agonized over my writing, but there was nothing I could do; the bone had to knit. Strange that one should describe what takes place in a fractured bone as "knitting," because it bears little resemblance to the activity of looping one stitch into another with a pair of pins or needles. Bone is constantly being created anew in the body through a complex process of resorption and renewal. As bone deteriorates it is carried away by cells called osteoclasts and is replaced with fresh bone by osteoblasts. When a bone is fractured as my humerus was—I could see it in the X rays, one piece protruding from the long smooth line, severed and moved aside—calluses of calcium form around it and then connect the two pieces. The repaired bone is often stronger than the original bone surrounding it, and the process of repair, like so many miracles of daily growth that occur in the body, is no doubt ingenious, but it's not what I would describe, by any stretch of the imagination, as knitting.

The healing took place in three stages. In the first stage I had to hold my arm immobile, hard against my side, while the calluses formed. Once I had become accustomed to the pain and had adjusted to doing everything with my left hand—one night I found myself in a Japanese restaurant manipulating chopsticks with my left hand with no idea when or how I had learned the skill — the game changed, and I had to learn how to move my arm again. The doctor showed me some simple exercises, which caused untold agony as I did them at home. My injury was close to the rotator cuff—a complex arrangement of muscles normally of little interest to anyone but major league pitchers—which meant that every part of my range of motion was affected and would have to be restored from scratch.

I am basically a lazy person, and there was nothing I would have liked better than to disobey the doctor's orders. However, it simply wasn't an option. There was no way I could choose to do without my right arm. So long as there was any way to salvage my range of motion and repair the damage, I had to give it my best effort. So I gritted my teeth and practiced the exercises while tears ran down my cheeks. Just as in martial arts, I was training not only my body but my psyche as well. I had to keep going and push through the pain, fighting my inner urgings to give up. This was a modus operandi that, though somewhat familiar to me, ran counter to all my natural instincts.

The doctor kept increasing the number of exercises I had to do. Later I would be going to physical therapy, but we weren't quite there yet. My arm was moving fairly well, if stiffly and painfully. "You'll need to do something to work the small muscles and keep them from atrophying," the doctor said. "Start exercising your hands."

Well. If there was one thing I knew how to do, it was exercise my hands. I was a knitter. Knitting had been an intermittent passion of mine for the past thirty years, ever since my college roommate, Debbie Kolb, taught me how to wield a pair of needles. I had taken to knitting like a duck to water and had probably devoted more time to it during my college years than to all my other studies combined.

I left the Boulevard of Broken Bones and went straight to Straw into Gold, a large Berkeley yarn store, to search out a suitable project. My heart was fairly dancing in my chest; for the first time in months I experienced joy and inspiration rather than just dogged determination to do what needed to be done. Set loose in a paradise of colors and textures, my mind reeling with possibilities, I wandered through the store, feeling the textures of the yarns, trying out one color after another in the mirror, paging through pattern books to see what caught my eye.

Often my inspiration to make something begins with a color. Many people believe that color itself has healing properties and that a strong attraction to a certain shade may reflect, as well as aesthetic preference, the body's need for a particular vibration. Clearly, color is transformative: the right one may light up a person's whole face, the wrong one cause her to disappear into the woodwork, or worse. Whether one chooses for reasons of health, beauty, or simple graphic impact, yarns offer a range and depth of colors rarely seen in ready-made clothes. On this day I fell in love with a velvety chenille in a deep shade of turquoise blue so vivid and intense it could have been painted by Maxfield Parrish in the just-before-twilight sky. I paired it with a cardigan pattern. The ribbing required a dyed-to-match fine wool, which Straw into Gold didn't carry.

My daughter came over and helped me make a list of every knitting store in the area, and then we started phoning around. I found what I was looking for in San Francisco and drove over to pick it up. By now I was as excited as I remembered being several years earlier, when Sam Kolb, Debbie's son, brought me a knitting project from his mother and I began knitting again after a long drought. I couldn't believe the pleasure I experienced.

"Wow!" I told Sam. "A reason to live!"

"You're worse than my mother," he said. "Even she doesn't knit first thing in the morning. You need to join Women Who Knit Too Much."

Sometimes a single color can expand into an entire universe. The chenille, which reminded me of the fine blue turquoise of Native American jewelry, had a natural affinity with silver. I had a set of Navajo silver buttons I had purchased from a local trading post some months earlier. I started my sweater with high excitement, envisioning the beauty of the finished product. I was dreaming of the velvet blouses trimmed with hundreds of silver buttons that Dineh grandmothers wear; in my mind's eye I saw them bathed in that burnished light that reflects off the red rock of the Southwest, set against the crisp blue of the desert sky.

My old friend Tamara called me. "I had a dream about you last night," she said. "You were wearing some sort of red calico outfit, with a long skirt. You were at Four Corners. You were waving at me. And your arm was fine, all healed."

"I'm knitting again," I said. "The doctor told me to exercise my hands. I bought this turquoise yarn that reminds me of the Southwest. Do you think I'm going there?"

Looking back, it seems peculiar that I even asked her that question. I had no particular interest in going to the Southwest, didn't know where Four Corners was, and didn't feel much like traveling. I thought I'd rather stay home and knit.

But I had a small problem, difficult to resolve. I was one button short of the number I needed to complete my sweater. The store where I had bought them had no more in stock. You wonder at the depths of my obsession? It didn't seem at all unreasonable to me to travel all the way to Arizona in the back of a pickup truck to shop for a single silver button.

CHAPTER THREE

Transfiguration of the Blues

As MY ARM HEALED, I had time to reflect on the various lessons I had learned in decades as a craftswoman and on the skills I still was lacking. At the time I started the turquoise chenille sweater, I had been knitting on and off for thirty years and was tired of being disappointed with the results. My finished sweaters rarely looked like the appealing pictures in the pattern books; or they came out looking like the pictures but didn't fit me; or they looked like the pictures and fit me, but in them I didn't resemble the models who wore them.

There was always some disappointment, frustration, heartache, or disillusionment attached to the knitting. Once in a yarn shop I overheard a beginner come upon the book *Knitting Without Tears* and wonder about its title. "What do tears have to do with knitting?" she wanted to know. "Keep knitting," I thought to myself. "You'll find out."

You might well ask why, after all this time, I had neither gotten to the bottom of my difficulties nor stopped knitting altogether. The answer is that I found the activity itself so intensely pleasurable and the process of putting together and starting a new project so immensely exhilarating that I went back to knitting time and again, hoping for better results.

Just as with love, each time I hoped it would be different.

The uncertainty I describe here is a central dilemma of craft in general. Since you are dealing with something you construct from scratch, you can never be sure what your project will look like in the end. Unless you are an expert fitter or tailor, which few of us are, you probably want to rely upon the skills of various pattern makers, thinking they have already done the job. It is always tempting to slavishly follow the pattern in a book, exactly as written, and dispense with the painstaking measurements, tedious mathematical calculations, and various decisions that must be made—all of which can become tiresome. We are, after all, impatient creatures who prefer our fantasies to harsh reality.

It's true that the pattern maker has done some of the work, but it is also essential that you contribute your part. If you take a gauge (stitches and rows per inch) and plan your garment with the aid of a schematic sketch (a diagram with measurements), you can reasonably predict the finished size. But you can't predict details or idiosyncrasies or a glitch in any one of the hundred aspects of putting together a handmade piece of clothing that will cause you either to love or hate the final result.

From hard experience I've been forced to concede that if I don't take the initiative to at least customize each pattern, if not design the sweater from scratch, I'll never get the results I imagine, except possibly with extreme good fortune and/or an expert designer, both occurring with the same frequency.

I've known many home sewers who stopped making clothing because it never fit properly or looked like what they envisioned. This same disappointment and frustration discourage many knitters who otherwise would love to pursue the craft. Unfortunately, the only cures for it are patience, love of the activity for its own self rather than for the end product, and a kind of rigorously honest self-knowledge that is difficult to achieve. It takes years to acquire a true sense of what we look like rather than what we wished we looked like and to know what we can and cannot wear. Why didn't I look like Natalie Wood in the sweater she had modeled? You'd be surprised how long it took me to figure out the answer to that question.

I had already begun taking the steps to resolve these dilemmas several years before my fall. After a long absence from knitting, I had taken up my needles again. My first effort, though restoring the love of the act to me almost immediately, had to be given away, as neither the color nor the style nor the fabric suited me in any way. After that I decided that I would no longer knit garments I couldn't wear. I got lucky with my next pattern, a cornflower blue cardigan I made from a Nancy Vale pattern. Nancy Vale is the knitwear designer responsible for Ralph Lauren's collection of so-called Navajo sweaters (a wonderful construct but rather a fantasy, as Navajos don't knit), which became popular in the early eighties as accessories for the Southwestern or prairie look. Beefy cardigans or vests with Fair Isle motifs, the sweaters were beautiful, and Nancy Vale's knitting instructions were better than most.

I learned several valuable lessons while knitting this blue sweater, but the most important was that knitting could be a balm for grief and pain. At the time I started knitting it, I had just ended a relationship with a man I deeply loved, and the grief I felt at his departure set off an episode of lower back troubles I had had for years. In emotional and physical distress, I found that knitting both distracted me from the pain and helped to heal my aching heart. It seemed as though I drew the blues out of my body and wove them into the texture of my sweater, exorcising them like a singer easing sorrow with a song.

This works for some knitters though not for others. Following the deaths of several people close to her in a short period of time, a woman I know sat in her sunny garden for months and constructed an immensely complicated Kaffe Fassett jacket. Kaffe Fassett is the California-born painter whose knitting designs, layering different colors and textures in visual blocks of elaborate complexity, have brought him world renown. Upon completing this demanding project, the woman felt not only that she had helped herself heal from the losses but also that she had somehow memorialized the people she loved in the finished "coat of many colors." Another woman I know found herself completely unable to knit following the death of her grown daughter. "I can't do it," she said, "because when I knit I think, and I don't want to think now; it's just too painful."

I am reminded of Tita, the main character in *Like Water for Chocolate*, who, when her lover is married to her sister, tries to get through her sleepless, heartbroken nights by knitting a bedspread. The depth of her sorrow is such that by the time she leaves home, following a nervous breakdown, the bedspread is so large and heavy that it won't fit inside the carriage.

> Tita grabbed it so tightly that there was no choice but to let it drag behind the carriage like the huge train of a wedding gown that stretched for a full kilometer. Tita used any yarn she happened to have in her bedspread, no matter what the color, and it revealed a kaleidoscopic combination of colors, textures, and forms that appeared and disappeared as if by magic in the gigantic cloud of dust that rose up behind it.

Recently I came across a passage in *A Whole New Life*, Reynolds Price's book about his horrifying bout with spinal cancer, that confirmed for me what I had experienced while knitting my way through grief and physical pain. "Again I am reminded of a home truth," he wrote, "that chronic pain sufferers sometimes forget—the fact that a thorough immersion in absorbing and, if possible, nonstop activity is far more narcotic than any drug."

My blue cardigan turned out to be wearable and even quite serviceable, if not exactly as beautiful as the picture, which seemed, upon reflection, to have contained at least one deliberate deception. The sleeves, which looked normal in the photograph, were almost bell-like when knitted according to the pattern. This is a particular dislike of mine; I make the sleeves smaller in almost everything I knit, because I don't like hauling around great heaps of fabric when I do things with my arms such as reaching for a cup of coffee. If I had been then the sort of knitter I aspire to being now, I might have ripped out the sleeves and redone them. I could have, but I didn't. Still the sweater fit in every other respect so well that I continue to use its basic measurements as a template for other sweaters.

This brings me to what I call the sweater reference library. Over the years as my knitting and wardrobe have accumulated, I have found that certain garments have elements that work especially well: the neckline on this one, the shoulders on that, the length on another, and so on. Unfortunately, these good parts seldom occur within the same garment. I gather up these orphans-with-one-good-quality and use them for my reference library. I have one old sweater I'll probably never fit into again in this lifetime, but the sleeves are almost perfect for me, so I model my sleeves on them. The blue cardigan has a good length and width; I often refer to and copy those measurements. Occasionally I find a pattern I like so much I knit it more than once. I use the previous version to model or alter what I did and didn't like. In knitting, I have found, nothing is ever really wasted.

❧

Creativity and inspiration are such mysterious processes, so much in the nature of gifts from the heavens, that the means we employ to find them are often bizarrely idiosyncratic. Sometimes I feel a particular kind of depression where I just lose interest in everything I normally like. I've identified this state of mind as a hunger of the imagination, my imagination's overwhelming and unsatisfied need for something to seize onto for inspiration. In my case this ennui can be cured most effectively by a visit to a fabric or yarn store. I much prefer to assemble the materials for a project, to fantasize and envision how it will look when it is completed, than to procure the finest finished product, though I occasionally have come across knitting or beadwork so fine that I longed with all my heart to possess it. This is the positive aspect of the craft conundrum I described before: the work lives and thrives in your imagination for a long time, providing pleasure and excitement far beyond its usefulness when finished.

I often describe myself as someone with a low bore-dom threshold, which is one reason I like to knit, as my passion is portable and may be performed anywhere. It never fails to amaze me that such a simple and often frus-trating activity has managed to hold my interest for so many years while other seemingly more compelling at-tractions have come and gone without leaving a trace.

Sometimes the simplest things are the most difficult to learn. I spent years simply getting my stitches to a fairly uniform size and my tension right. Nothing else. I'm hes-itant to admit just how long it took me to find out that I had to fit my sweaters to the measurements of my own body, and even then I didn't figure it out myself; my mother had to tell me.

My mother knits without a pattern, which is like flying on a trapeze without a net. As knitters we have different strengths. She prefers to use the same weight of wool and size of needle over and over, and she designs everything to fit her measurements and whatever her whim of the moment. She sometimes begins knitting without know-ing what the finished product will turn out to be. Unlike me, my mother is always pleased with her final results and wears her sweaters proudly, all the time. However, she does not know how to read or follow a pattern and marvels at the way I switch from one complicated design to another, with different sized needles and yarns that vary from cotton to wool to linen to cashmere.

In early 1990 I was visiting my parents in Florida, in the house they owned near the horse country in southwest Broward County. I usually knitted in a rocking chair near the pool, in a little lounge area my mother had set up for me. Buoyed up by the success of my blue cardigan, I had embarked on another Nancy Vale pattern, using a shiny mercerized cotton yarn in my then-favorite shade: a vivid teal green, the color of a mallard's neck feathers. The style was portrayed with an impressionistic sketch rather than a photograph, so I really had no idea what it was going to look like. I had knitted about six inches of the pattern when my mother came out to see what I had done. It looked like something that would be tight on a waif .

"What, are you kidding?" my mother said. "That will never fit you in a million years." Then she showed me how to measure myself around the bust and multiply the number of stitches in the gauge (in this case five stitches to the inch) by my bust measurement to make the sweater fit. I used a pretty and delicate willow-twig stitch I found in an old knitting magazine in her collection and modified the sweater by adding a few extra inches for ease. Since it was going to be far too wide at the shoulders, and because I am partial to yokes, we came up with the idea for a ribbed yoke to pull in the fabric. The results were the best I had ever achieved, and the sweater was truly mine. I wear it to this day; it reminds me of the invaluable lesson my mother taught me, a simple basic that utterly transformed my knitting, the craft equivalent of "To thine own self be true."

In the old days when needlework was taught in families and schools, there was always an older and more accomplished knitter you could go to with your questions and concerns. All crafts are passed not in an oral but in a tactile tradition where you learn with your hands and by your own mistakes and the better example of someone else; as a rule it is difficult to learn a craft from books. Just as creativity is one of the highest forms of human expression, it seems equally true that it is our duty to pass on what we know to future generations so that the precious knowledge, hard-won and painstakingly accumulated, will not be lost.

Although my college roommate had taught me initially how to knit and purl, I could always go to my mother with my problems and dilemmas. I remember making a royal blue wool turtleneck quite early in my knitting career and being in despair because it came out too small. "Give it to me," my mother said. "I'll block it." My mother liked to do her ironing and mending late at night when the house was quiet. I went to bed. In the morning my mother handed me the blue sweater, which now fit perfectly. Through a mysterious process of steaming and stretching, she had made the bumpy and uneven stitches look smooth and uniform and had changed my garment into something I could wear.

In *War and Peace* there is a scene that illustrates some of the homegrown magic that seems to attach to the humble craft of knitting.

> "Anna Makarovna has finished her stocking," said Countess Marya. . . . They meant two stockings, which, by a secret known only to her, Anna Makarovna used to knit on her needles simultaneously. When the pair was finished, she always made a solemn ceremony of pulling one stocking out of the other in the presence of the children.

There is always something magical in the process of knitting, although the products that come from it are so ordinary in our lives (socks, shawls, blankets, sweaters) that we give little thought to how they are made. The very fact of making something three-dimensional out of a basically flat piece of yarn (let alone the spinning and all the shearing, carding, and dyeing that preceded it) is in itself as dazzling as a conjure trick. In essence, nothing could be simpler than looping one loop inside another over and over until a fabric of extraordinary pliability and elasticity has been achieved, but to those not initiated into its mysteries, the sight of the flying hands and disappearing wool and the finished garment that emerges from the needles are as baffling and unexpected as the rabbit that pops from the magician's hat.

CHAPTER FOUR

A Life
Made by Hand

As a child I longed for a cloak that would make me invisible. For a woman, middle age is that cloak. I hear this idea expressed in different ways: "I have reached the age of invisibility." "No one seems to notice me anymore." And so on. This is both a blessing and a bane. At long last, after serving as a magnet for men and a vessel for reproduction, we finally own our lives again. We can go about our business unmolested, free to be who we are rather than who others want or need us to be. We are persons again, as we haven't been since we were prepubescent girls. The disadvantage is that even when we want to be noticed, we probably won't be.

In a culture that places so much emphasis on the attainment and maintenance of physical beauty, this can be devastating. For a woman used to the attentions of men, intimate friends as well as strangers, sudden invisibility can come as a depressing shock. I found in early menopause that I had to grieve for my youth and beauty and ability to reproduce; these were losses that had to be felt and acknowledged before I could let them go.

It soon became clear that it was time to construct a whole new identity, one that could carry me for the next twenty or so years into old age. Just as we have to forge a new identity at puberty, to prepare for adulthood and entering the world of women, and again when we give birth to children, this need also recurs with menopause. The puberty transition seems to force us into a false self, one that will be both pleasing to our parents and teachers and sexually alluring, while the motherhood self is one adopted for the benefit of others rather than for ourselves. Menopause may be the first time in our lives when we are free to discover who we really are, away from the disapproving eyes of society, which makes it abundantly clear it no longer needs us.

How do we, who have always been in the service of others, discover an authentic self?

In the book *Women's Bodies, Women's Wisdom,* Dr. Christiane Northrup tells the story of Peggy, a fifty-eight-year-old kindergarten teacher who, with the coming of menopause, lost her ability to concentrate in the classroom.

> She left school, traveled to California, and lived in a small cottage near the beach for a year. During that time, she began to knit. She found that the knitting was exactly what her brain needed for meditative activity.
>
> On a hunch, Peggy began to teach senior citizens the knitting techniques she was learning. She mailed a beach chair to me. She had handknit the seat and the back in beautiful and unusual designs. She found that her skills were in great demand. . . . By the time I saw her a year later, she was a healed woman with a great deal of trust in life. She had accepted the challenge of menopause, moved into her intuitive side, and begun a whole new life.

Although I am a knitter, I went about my menopause transformation in a slightly different way. As I was both fatigued and insomniac (they go together, don't they?), I spent a lot of time sitting still. I had to think about what I wanted from life, what qualities would now become important to me and hopefully would replace the ones I was losing. I was strongly opposed to taking estrogen for a variety of reasons, not least of which is that many indigenous medicine people, such as the native Hawaiian kahunas, view a woman past menopause as having attained or being capable of a higher level of spiritual clarity. The blood you no longer lose with menstruation is regarded as "wise blood," which stays inside and nourishes a kind of wisdom and inner power, qualities that now seemed intensely desirable to me. Without going into a detailed discussion of hormone replacement therapy, I will say here that I personally was deterred by the prospect of continuing to bleed and wondered if the artificial prolonging of a youthful state might not short-circuit the psychic and spiritual reward I anticipated at the end of the uncomfortable physical transition. I thought a lot during this time about attributes like presence and mastery and cultivated a certain indifference to the ebb and flow of emotional problems, which suddenly seemed the province of the young.

I have always loved to make things with my hands and for the whole of my life have admired craftspeople capable of making remarkable beauty out of objects required for everyday life. I particularly loved Native American beadwork. It spoke to me in a way no fine art ever had. I believe I related to those tribal craftswomen empathetically through the work of their hands. I had always wanted to do beadwork and began to teach myself. My friend Tamara had given me a small kit for Christmas, which contained embroidery floss for duplicating in cross-stitch some imaginatively rendered patterns adapted from antique Indian blankets and fabric for fashioning the embroidered pieces into tiny pillows filled with herbs.

I am not a moderate person, so there was no way I could do one of these and stop. Soon I was researching Navajo blanket patterns and translating them into minia-ture embroidered pouches backed with chamois and lined with calico. I was also beading on the chamois, teaching myself, as that was the only way I knew, strug-gling to imitate some of the woodland floral patterns I had especially admired.

Natalie Goldberg once observed, in *Writing Down the Bones*, that when you start to write, unseen forces in the universe appear to help you. This has also happened to me with crafts. The sensation is almost impossible to de-scribe, as it occurs through the hands rather than the mind and is utterly nonverbal in nature, but it feels as though invisible teachers were guiding your movements. Perhaps it is not that at all but merely a connection to the collective unconscious or a kind of ancestral memory common to us all, where those types of knowledge are stored. You don't know it's there until you tap into it by accident, with a particular motion of the hands, and then suddenly, with an almost electric shock, the body re-members.

An article I read in *Knitter's Magazine* described Elizabeth Zimmermann, one of the three best-known knitters in the United States (along with Barbara Walker and Meg Swansen), crafting, in 1957, the first Aran sweater pattern published in *Vogue Knitting*. She had taken the unbleached woolen yarn and her needles on a camping trip to the Mississippi River.

> While her husband fished, she sat in the boat and knitted. "I puzzled over the directions," she later wrote in *Knitter's Almanac*, "which included no picture of what I was actually making. . . . The oiled wool slipped through my fingers . . . the sun beat down upon it all, and thus the dream began . . . a strong feeling that my fingers knew quite well what they were about. . . . I knew then that I had been through this before, with younger fingers in a ruder boat, rocked on the salty summer waves of the Atlantic off the Irish coast."

It seems entirely possible to me that the human hand, which is such a marvel of nature and which contains the opposable thumb so important in our evolution as a species, has its own form of intelligence and memory. I have certainly experienced memory in my hands while cooking and also the quality of mastery, a kind of casual excellence achieved without conscious effort. The concept of kinesthetic intelligence, while coming closest, does not do justice to this extraordinary phenomenon.

As I worked with the Navajo rug weaving patterns— the cross symbolizing the four directions, the zigzag for lightning sent by the Thunder Beings, and so on—I absorbed some aspect of the culture into my psyche through my hands. You learn about a culture differently when working, as opposed to looking at, a pattern; you form an affinity on a deeper level of being. Some part of your consciousness grasps purely and empathetically the mind-set of the person who created the design. I know from doing certain types of meditation that consciousness understands a language of colors, abstract symbols, and forms; it also understands basic sounds, like those of the Sanskrit seed syllables (*Om*, etc.), rather than a verbal and cerebral depiction of the universe. This is nothing new, only a statement of fact known to mystics in every tradition.

Years ago when I began reading about Native American spirituality in, for instance, *Black Elk Speaks*, I was struck by how closely American Indian mysticism paralleled Tibetan Buddhism in the use of colors, directions, and some of the same basic explanations for our inexplicable and ultimately mysterious cosmos. Mad Bear, the late Tuscarora medicine man, active in the American

Indian Movement for many years, claimed that this was because Tibetans and Indians were originally the same people, from the same root stock. I like to think it's also because the sacred parts of humanity's knowledge—the dharma, as the Tibetans call it—contain universal elements that have been preserved and understood from one culture and historical time to another because the information is objective: true and unchanging.

As above, so below; the inside mirrors the outside, and vice versa; ontogeny recapitulates phylogeny on almost every level of existence, from the cellular to the behavioral, and so as I worked with beads and the patterns of Navajo weaving, I connected with spiritual ancestors inside me, and my inner life seemed to attract an outer landscape to match.

∞

I had spent the summer before I broke my arm in South Dakota, visiting Indian Country. I went to the Badlands, to the Black Hills, and to Bear Butte, *Mato Paha*, a mountain sacred to both the Lakota and Northern Cheyenne. Sweet Medicine, the spiritual leader of the Cheyenne, was said to have received the four Sacred Arrows on Bear Butte, and to this day it is a site for vision quests. Tobacco ties and prayer flags in the colors of the four directions hang from the trees, and a large part of the mountain, a volcanic laccolith, is off limits to whites. "Indians praying. Do not pass beyond this point," reads a sign limiting access on one of the paths. The presence of spirits and spiritual power on Bear Butte is strong and unmistakable, a force to be reckoned with and approached with grave respect.

As much as I could, I was following in the footsteps of Crazy Horse, the legendary Oglala Sioux chief, a long-time hero of mine, not least because he followed the dictates of his own heart and spirit. He fought against the coming of a way of life whose disastrous effects, in the form of environmental degradation, we are struggling to cope with today. The Native Americans' view of the earth and of their relatedness to all living things, in what ecologists would later call "the indivisible world," had much to do with the way they practiced their handcrafts. As Peter Matthiessen put it in *Indian Country*, our society's "lunatic insistence on 'progress,' on 'growth,' on gross national product . . . is destroying the land and air and water, the wild animals and plants . . . not to speak of quality and craftsmanship, birdsong, silence, night, and the very soul of man."

In midlife it begins to feel terribly urgent to us that we attend to the things that will nurture our soul, on an individual as well as a societal level. "Technology is going to destroy the human soul," the folksinger Pete Seeger said recently, "unless we realize that each of us must in some way be a creator as well as a spectator or consumer." As a society we are desperately in search of a better, more spiritual way to live; our very survival as a species depends upon it. For myself, at this time I needed to find different heroes, new archetypes on which to model myself, authentic values I could live by, a lost world I might regain through the work of my hands.

Crazy Horse was murdered at Fort Robinson, Nebraska, in 1877, because he could not accept imprisonment after being promised safe passage and his own reservation if he would bring his starving band in from the wild. After his death, his grieving parents buried his heart and bones separately at secret sites where they could rest undisturbed. Some say his heart is buried near Wounded Knee Creek, others that his bones lie in the Badlands or somewhere on Bear Butte. Black Elk said that it didn't matter where his bones were, "but where his spirit is, that would be a good place to be."

The cavalry had pursued Crazy Horse's band, as they did many others, through the brutal winter. The soldiers would surprise a sleeping camp, scatter the women and children, and set fire to the lodges, the clothing, the stores of winter food. Food and lodging were matters of life or death; yet perhaps no less precious were the ceremonial objects contributing to spiritual survival. I sometimes wondered how the women felt seeing their precious handwork go up in smoke, the painstaking hours and months of tanning the hides and trading for the beads and beading the designs on the moccasins, cradleboards, pipe bags, and buffalo robes, all lost forever.

Traveling through South Dakota, I had visited as many collections of beadwork as I could, and once back in Minneapolis, I attended a class at the Indian Cultural Center hoping to learn some tricks for doing floral beadwork embroidery from the Chippewa women teaching it. I did; it has to be done with two needles, one for making the design, one for anchoring it to the leather. I still haven't mastered it but am hopeful that someday I will.

The stunning landscape of the Great Plains, the great empty spaces to the horizon, the palette of spring green and sky blue, the low-lying clouds casting shadows on the land, the song of the meadowlark at every turn, the sense of the past and whisperings of ancestors whose bones lay hidden beneath the grass—all provided a rich banquet for my eyes and imagination. It's always difficult to pinpoint the precise source of inspiration; by the time your experience has sifted down through all the layers of consciousness to emerge as art or craft, the original spark may well be forgotten. But I know that inspiration was what I was looking for, and that was what I found.

It all went together for me—the land, the beadwork, the sacred sites, the history, the heroes and archetypes, the inner life that accommodated them all. I spent a lot of time in writing and contemplation, thinking about what I wanted for the next phase of my life. It was a quiet, introspective time, a time for reflection and regrouping, for exploring who I really was inside. In *Women Who Run with the Wolves*, Clarissa Pinkola Estés writes about how intentional solitude can nourish the soul. I was fashioning a new life for myself, according to my own models and to suit my own needs, and, like the crafts I was making, it was going to have to be made by hand.

CHAPTER FIVE

Spider Woman's Daughters

SOMETIMES KNITTING TAKES YOU on an inner journey; sometimes it takes you on an outer one. My turquoise chenille sweater, which had been inspired by visions of Dineh grandmothers in their velvet blouses with silver buttons, ended up leading me on a trip through Navajo country, where the real-life grandmothers lived. I thought I was looking for a silver button, but of course I found much more.

For several years I had been doing volunteer work at a Native American drug and alcohol treatment center in my community. Over time I became friends with one of the counselors there, a Navajo named Jimmy Woodbine (name changed to protect privacy). We shared an interest in hummingbirds and a compatible sense of humor. When I appeared at the center with my right arm broken and told Jimmy how I had followed a hummingbird off a deck, he roared with laughter.

Later that night he took me to see his uncle, Guy Manybeads, a medicine man who was visiting from Monument Valley. Guy spoke only Navajo, which sounded to my ear like a cross between Chinese and German, and Jimmy translated. Despite the language barrier, a lot of good-natured joking and teasing went on before we got down to the serious business of doctoring, and the three of us ended up spending quite a bit of time together before Guy had to go back home.

A few weeks after he had gone, Jimmy asked if I wanted to go with him to Arizona and Utah to get some further treatment for my arm. I was wary of traveling so far with my arm in so fragile a condition; I would be riding in the back bed of a camper truck the whole way. But I had grown fond of Guy and wanted to see him again, and I knew that this trip was the opportunity of a lifetime; with Jimmy I would have access to places where I could never go alone. What cinched the decision for me, however, was knowing that I could find the missing button for my sweater at one of the trading posts on the Big Reservation. So I packed in a hurry and hit the road with Jimmy.

We traveled in a red Toyota camper. I sat in the back and knitted while Jimmy drove. He played Native American Church peyote songs on the tape deck; the pulsing rattle, hypnotic beat of the water drum, and steady high-pitched singing accompanied us through all the thousands of miles we drove and set the rhythm of my stitches as I worked.

As my knitting progressed, I noticed something peculiar about the pattern I was following. After I had knitted what I thought looked like normal armholes on the back of the sweater, the instructions said to continue on for another sixty rows or so. I called my mother. "I don't know," she said. "I never make my armholes longer than nine inches. I think you better stop."

I don't know what frame of mind I was in, some sort of magical thinking, but I ignored my own instincts and my mother's advice and went on as the pattern suggested until the sweater was grotesquely out of proportion, imagining that some sort of mysterious trick would make it come right in the end. I just held onto my vision of silver buttons on turquoise velvet and trudged gamely on.

As countless writers familiar with the craft have found, the way a person knits can speak volumes about that person's character. My favorite example of this is Louise Erdrich's description of pregnant, feisty, redheaded Dot Adare in *Love Medicine*:

> The child rode high, and she often rested her forearms on it while she knitted. One of Dot's most peculiar feats was transforming that gentle task into something perverse. She knit viciously, jerking the yarn around her thumb until the tip whitened, pulling each stitch so tightly that the little garments she finished stood up by themselves like miniature suits of mail.

A novelist might say about me during this time that I was knitting unconsciously, caught in a trance between two worlds. The fall that broke my arm both had started me knitting again and had set in motion the chain of events that now found me seated cross-legged in the bed of a red pickup truck in Arizona, blithely leaving behind common sense and heading toward an obviously huge knitting mistake. I was on my way to somewhere, toward a new way of knowing myself and my craft, but I hadn't quite arrived there yet. This particular glaring error would do much to advance me toward that end, but like all valuable lessons it would prove to be costly.

The buttes and spires of Monument Valley rise up out of a landscape of so vast a sweep that it seems a place where God himself (herself?) could take a walk. As we drove into Monument Valley, a rich silence unfolded around us, and I drank in the beauty of the desert palette—ochre, carnelian, sage green, lavender, and deep sky blue—that colors this visionary country.

Guy Manybeads lived with a woman I'll call Tillie in a trailer off a side road. Jimmy and I stayed in a nearby campground and visited the trailer so Guy could doctor my arm. As I was soon to find out, almost all Navajo women have a loom at home with a rug in progress; Tillie's was hidden behind a curtain in the bedroom of the trailer.

Part of a medicine person's responsibility involves being totally available to treat anyone at any time and to be willing to travel to wherever they are. So while we were on the big reservation, Jimmy and I often spent our time chasing Guy around to various places or driving him here and there to do his work.

One day we followed him to Big Mountain, down past the Hopi mesas and up a dirt road so bumpy and rutted that I thought the bottom would be torn from the truck.

We arrived late at night and parked with other campers and pickups in a circle around a roaring bonfire.

The scene that greeted my eyes the next morning was among the most foreign I have ever witnessed. Jerry-built wooden structures roofed with bright blue tarps formed a series of rooms open on one side like a dollhouse. Before portable cookstoves in front, a long line of women stood patting dough and slapping it back and forth between their hands for frybread. Many of the women wore traditional Navajo clothing: long tiered skirts, rust-colored moccasins with white soles and silver fastenings, velvet blouses decorated with silver buttons and large silver and turquoise brooches, and a varied assortment of ornate bracelets, necklaces, earrings, and belts. Some of the older women wore kerchiefs over their hair; others had theirs wrapped with yarn in the bun, or *tsiyeel*, worn by both men and women.

Behind the shacks, more women were butchering sheep, expertly skinning off the white curly fleece, systematically cleaning the long lines of intestines by drawing them through their fingers, then wrapping them around their hands. Men chopped and hauled wood for the cookstoves and bonfires. Every activity was accompanied by the bleating of sheep, penned up and waiting to be slaughtered for food. More trucks kept arriving with sheep in their beds, along with large sacks of flour and cases of soda.

Guy had brought us to a ceremony, or sing, that would be held over the next few days. Like Madame deFarge in *A Tale of Two Cities*, who encoded the crimes of the French aristocrats in her endless knitting, I tried to record everything I heard and saw at the Navajo encampment in my turquoise chenille cardigan.

We were on Big Mountain, site of the so-called land dispute between the Hopi and Navajo and the largest proposed relocation of a civilian population since the internment of the Japanese in World War II. Big Mountain is primarily sheepherding country, a stronghold of the traditional Dineh way of life, and many of the people in the camp were activists in the fight against relocation.

Navajo women live by the proceeds of their yarn and their craft. The women of Big Mountain have supported their struggle to stay on the land largely with the aid of a weaving project. Daughters of Spider Woman, who, according to Dineh cosmology, brought weaving to the people, teaching men how to construct the standing looms and women how to use them, Navajo women inherit the land their families live on and have always commanded good money for their highly prized blankets and rugs. Navajo mothers bury the umbilical cords of their babies beneath the looms and livestock corrals to point the lives of their children in a good direction.

There is a further dimension to the weaving as well. In *The View from the Mesa*, Shonto Begay describes watching her mother weave. "The spiritual connection she pushed down with every row wove her deeper into the heart of the pattern," she writes. Though the rugs are varied, with the women's styles differing according to region and individual preference, all Navajo blankets have one thing in common. Somewhere in the design will appear a thin line, incompatible with the rest of the pattern, reaching to the edge of the rug. This is known as the spirit path, by which the weaver travels out of the rug so that she may go on to create more. Without it, her spirit might become trapped in the blanket. This sort of intentional imperfection is a common tradition in the construction of many aboriginal crafts.

As a knitter, I was fascinated by this information and by the sheep-based culture of the traditional Navajo, who rely on wool to bring them what they need from the outside world. "We have only our shuttles and yarn to make a living," one Big Mountain weaver told a newspaper reporter.

All the Navajo women I met shared a quality I have noticed in Native American women time and again, a kind of solidity and presence that has to do with their sense of belonging to a place. It was something that I wished I could learn from them and that I had tried to cultivate in myself through the practice of crafts. I was looking for a kind of rootedness, an interconnectedness with the earth, a way of being at home. Home is something that my people have not had much luck with for at least the past few millennia, scattered all over the globe as we are in the Jewish Diaspora.

I have always believed that the physical land you inhabit draws you into it and imbues you with its own qualities, whether you want it to or not, but that's a different matter from actively belonging to the land and the land to you.

Because of the vast array of cultures and tribes that make up the indigenous peoples of the Americas, no single way of looking at the world can be characterized as Native American. Yet some common beliefs appear in the systems of various tribes. One is that the whole world is alive, composed of spirit, and needs to be approached with gratitude, reverence, and respect. Another is the traditionals' view of time: the past is not gone and firmly out of the way but rather is alive in us in the present, as are the lives of our ancestors and their experience of the world. Whether this can best be described as an awareness that lives in the blood, as ancestral memories, or even as the collective unconscious, I do not know, only that it is powerfully affecting, cutting to the bone of who we are.

I knew something of the inner lives of the Navajo women because in making my own crafts I had in a sense entered some of their designs, calculating the measurements necessary to achieve the desired proportions and living with the symbols and the patterns as they passed through my hands.

The difference was that they had a culture they expressed through their crafts, while I was actively looking for mine. The knitting project I had brought with me would mark the last time I blindly followed a pattern as it was written down without putting myself into the design. And, as has happened so often to travelers in foreign lands, the shock of being in an unfamiliar environment helped me discover more deeply just who exactly I was. My experience of being on the Navajo reservation heightened my sense of my own Jewishness. Watching the generations of extended families working and praying and celebrating together made me miss my own far-flung clan with a pain so acute that I broke down in tears. My awareness that the Big Mountain families' continued survival on this land was severely threatened was another source of pain. I had seen firsthand the results of cultural and geographic dislocation on the populations of urban

Indians I worked with at the treatment center and, more intimately, in my own psyche.

Guy had told me that I broke my arm because I had fallen out of harmony with the natural world. I was now in the process of learning how I could salve that sense of dislocation I felt. By expressing my culture—everything I had been born into and had gathered on my own— through the work of my hands, I was trying to bring myself back into harmony and healing, creating a home inside myself and learning to inhabit more fully the home we shared in common on the earth.

One night a squaw dance, done in a circle, was held as part of the ceremony. Women had to ask men to dance, and men had to pay money to ransom their way out. There is a Sufi exercise called *zikr* that is also done as a dance. The whirling dervishes perform it as they turn in circles, repeating the sacred names of God until they are drawn into ecstatic union with the Divine. I danced with Jimmy and with Guy in the circle and afterward had the distinct impression that we had been performing *zikr* Navajo style.

Although I am not a religiously observant Jew, some facets of my being spring deeply from my Jewish origins, such as my craving for mystical transcendence. The Baal Shem Tov himself, founder of Hasidism, the most rapturous mystical element of Judaism, liked to go out in the woods and dance his joy in the creation, a celebration of spirituality that runs as a common thread through many cultures and traditions. Jews are known as People of the Book, yet somewhere inside myself I crave more deeply a communion with nature, with palpable works that emanate from the hands of God. I am a woman. Like old-time nuns embroidering priests' vestments in the convents of Belgium or Navajo women weaving blankets in their hogans, I know how to pray with my hands. And I need for those prayers to connect me to earth.

Guy Manybeads was always telling me I should learn to speak Dineh, move to Arizona, and be adopted into the Navajo tribe. Once when Jimmy and I had returned from a trip to Colorado, he embraced me warmly in the kitchen of the trailer and said, "I'm so glad you have come home."

I wasn't physically at home on the Navajo reservation, but I often felt comfortable and accepted, completely natural and at ease among a sisterhood of women who lived by their craft. The unified cycle of livelihood, art, and spirituality involved in the keeping of sheep and the processing of their fleece into products that both celebrated the Dineh cosmology and ensured economic survival seemed to provide the kind of relatedness I imagined existing in communities before the Industrial Revolution. If it was not altogether a worry-free paradise, it at least gave the appearance of being a more satisfyingly integrated society than the one we live in now. It was similar in quality to the lives of women on the Shetland and Aran Islands, with whom I also felt intimately acquainted through the common working out of patterns. I knitted constantly and hoped that something of the Navajo women's organic inspiration and rootedness would flow into me through my hands.

After Big Mountain, we drove around endlessly, seven thousand miles in three weeks. On one trip we passed through Four Corners, where New Mexico, Colorado, Arizona, and Utah meet, and stopped to take pictures. I thought of my friend Tamara's dream as I waved for the camera, my arm now vastly improved. Guy and Jimmy rode in the front of the Toyota, and I sat in the back, working on my turquoise sweater. Suddenly Guy, who was immensely proud of his military service in World War II, turned around and asked me if I came from the same people who had been murdered by the Germans in that war.

"Yes," I answered.

"Then you're not white," he said. "You're a Jew Indian."

"I guess that would make me a Navajew," I said. I was only half joking; it seemed like a truth. I felt as though I'd been reunited with one of the lost tribes of Israel and was traveling once more with my people after an overlong exile from home.

CHAPTER SIX

Winged Hearts

ON MY TRAVELS through the Navajo Nation I had knitted the back, both sleeves, and half the left front panel of my turquoise chenille cardigan. As I finished this panel at home, it became clear that the proportions were wrong and that I would have to rip out much of what I had knitted. The first thing that came to my mind was the framed sign that hangs in Greenwich Yarn in San Francisco: "As you knit, so shall you rip." I felt annoyed with the company that had published the pattern but angrier with myself for having followed it so blindly.

I resolved that the next time I knitted I would find a different way to work.

After I had reknit the sweater, my friend Karen fell in love with the finished product, borrowed it from my "reference library," and took it to the Knitting Basket to have it copied into a new pattern. The Knitting Basket is the high-end yarn store in our area and as a rule deals in luxury yarns from companies such as Missoni, Filatura de Crosa, and Rowan. They always carry the newest and the best of what's available in the handknitting world.

To give you a bit of background here, sometime in the late seventies the English company Rowan began to revolutionize the home knitting industry by publishing pattern books filled with stylish designs photographed on beautiful models (I first saw supermodel Kate Moss in a Rowan pattern book) in dreamy settings full of mystique and ambiance. The photographs promoted their line of yarns, available in an unusual range of sophisticated colors. Many of today's prominent knitwear designers—Annabel Fox, Kaffe Fassett, Edina Ronay—came out of the Rowan design family, and their imaginative patterns took knitting from the somewhat hokey province of eccentric old ladies to elegant bastions of hip modern style.

I used to spend a lot of time at the Knitting Basket browsing and I occasionally bought some specialty yarns there. I always made a beeline for bright, multicolored, shiny, tweedy yarns, and it took me years to discover that what I was knitting, the garish colors and bulky textures of the yarns, had almost nothing to do with the dark, plain, almost severe styles I liked to wear.

I had noticed, as well, that the women who worked at the Knitting Basket were far more accomplished at the craft than I and that they constructed garments of a dazzling complexity beyond my wildest dreams. An idea began to grow in my mind. It was obvious that I had been knitting long enough to have attained this level of proficiency; only my lack of commitment and confidence and an inability to ask for help were keeping me from it. I decided I wanted to become a master knitter, though I was vague about just what exactly that entailed. After all my years of messed-up projects and semifailures, it suddenly seemed terribly important to me to achieve mastery at something I had spent so many hours thinking about and doing.

The Knitting Basket carried a yarn I particularly coveted, a cashmere, silk, and merino wool blend, ultrafine and wildly expensive. Linda, the shop's owner, had made an impressive asymmetrical sweater heavily textured with cables, bobbles, and other fancy stitches from the yarn. I was afraid I couldn't afford it and couldn't knit well enough to justify the expense and was convinced I wouldn't like working on the smaller-sized needles it required. But I fell in love with the dark red color it came in. "I'll buy one ball and take it home to fool around with," I told Linda.

At home I knitted a sample swatch. I made up a pattern that looked like thin satin ribbons, separated by narrow panels of nubby seed stitch. The sensuous feel of the yarn sliding over my fingers was intensely pleasurable, a caress for my hands. I gathered up a bunch of old clothing and books and went out to sell them at secondhand stores. Then I returned to the Knitting Basket. "I knew you'd be back," said Linda. "Once you touch this yarn, it's almost impossible to resist."

I bought enough yarn to make a sweater and began poring through the pattern books, looking for something suitable. "I'm tired of making things that don't come out right," I complained to Linda. "The patterns don't fit or don't look like the pictures. I end up putting all this work into sweaters I don't like to wear. Aren't there any foolproof patterns?"

"Not really," said Linda. "It's always a crap shoot."

"Even for you?" I asked. I had come to regard her as the best knitter I had ever known. From a technical point of view, I thought Linda could walk on water.

"I rip a lot," she said casually. "And every time I start something, I know I'm taking my chances."

I appreciated her honesty. It made me feel like I wasn't alone. And that there was hope. If knitting were a gamble for Linda, and she still managed to come up with astonishing results, maybe I could learn to do the same.

∞

Linda suggested an Edina Ronay pattern for my red cashmere sweater. It had the right gauge and I liked the main cable that repeated in the design, but I didn't care for the overall shape. In fact I couldn't seem to find a pattern good enough for the yarn, nothing that looked like what I wanted. I had bought a hardbound book of Annabel Fox designs, one of which contained panels of embossed hearts. I took the cable from the Edina Ronay and the hearts from the Annabel Fox, put them together with the ribbon pattern I had come up with in my sample swatch, and roughed out a number of repetitions for the design. I called it "Heart on My Sleeve." I secretly name all my sweaters—"Hannah," "Mood Indigo," "Diamonds Are a Girl's Best Friend," "Skyglass," and so forth. It happens instinctively, without trying, a reflex; like making up headlines for the magazine articles I write.

∞

I was thinking a lot about hearts at that time because I had met an elderly *murshida,* or teacher, associated with the Sufi Order of the West, whose symbol is the heart with wings. Hayat, as she was called, was in her early nineties and lived not far from my neighborhood. I had gotten to know her through Tamara, who was one of her students. Hayat took to me because we both went to Vassar; she had graduated in the class of 1921.

At the time I met Hayat I was undergoing physical therapy for my arm. I'd been fortunate to find an acknowledged expert on rotator cuff injuries, but he was a hard taskmaster, and his massages were hard to bear.

"You could have worked for the Spanish Inquisition," I told him one day. "You know, renounce the one true God or we'll send you to physical therapy."

I went to my therapy sessions in the morning and had plenty of free time in the afternoon. Hayat began inviting me to her house for lunch. She lived in a small house near the Chapel of the Chimes in Oakland, where she had worked as chaplain, performing weddings and such, until her retirement over twenty years earlier. The interior of her house was painted a delicate shell pink, and, winter or summer, the heater was running full blast. The first thing many of her students did upon entering her house was to surreptitiously turn down the thermostat. Hayat herself was tiny, with little bird bones and mouselike facial features. Her fingers were knotted and bent with arthritis, and she had a funny way of moving, launching herself into a kind of propulsion rather than actually walking. She spoke so softly, barely above a papery whisper, that you had to lean close to hear what she was saying. She had both the smallest voice and the biggest heart of anyone I ever knew.

Lunch at Hayat's was usually Waldorf salad on red leaf lettuce with Thousand Island dressing, deviled eggs, cheese, toasted English muffin with jam, finished with tea and thin ginger cookies. Hayat on the whole seemed to eat barely enough to keep a flea alive; it was almost painful at times to embrace her fragile bones.

Before eating, we clasped hands, and she repeated a blessing: "O Thou, the sustainer of our bodies, hearts, and souls, bless all that we receive in thankfulness. Amen."

She was losing, in just about equal measure, her eyesight and hearing, so it was difficult to have a two-way conversation with Hayat. I much preferred, at any rate, to listen, rapt, to her reminiscences and sometimes wicked gossip. She tended to repeat herself; certain loops of thought went round more than once, and she indulged the prejudices of her class, but there was a quality in her talk that went beyond words. I often had the sensation, sitting at her table, that I continued to rise higher and

higher into the air as she spoke. The room would fill
with that rose-colored light from the walls, and I would
become weightless and pleasantly lightheaded. Driving
home from her house was often difficult; I had to fight to
pay attention to the road.

I adored being in her presence and was inspired, as
well, by what she had accomplished in her life. At the
time I was doing weekly *zikrs* with a more traditional Sufi
order, and Hayat disapproved of their rigid adherence to
Islamic form. She didn't think much of any sort of *zikr*.
"They have it all wrong," she would say. "Rumi danced
because his soul was on fire. He didn't set fire to it by
dancing." She liked to describe herself as "a free thinker,"
unbound by any tradition. She was in love with Gawd, as
she called the Creator, and she saw divinity everywhere.
"Everything is Gawd," she would exclaim delightedly
and then go on in the next breath to decry the awful
meaninglessness of abstract modern art or repeat some
sinfully delicious gossip about a mutual acquaintance.

For many years she had kept birds as pets. Although
they were all now dead, Tamara swore that she had seen
them flitting about the empty birdcages in the bedroom.
Hayat had written the life story of each of her birds in
a series she called "The Whimsies," and she liked to
describe their different personality traits. Birds figure
prominently in Sufi mythology, as in Attar's well-known

allegory "Parliament of the Birds." I had a friend who used to tell me stories from the Idries Shah collections, introducing each with the phrase "This one is for your bird," meaning my soul. But Hayat had a unique relationship with winged creatures, almost as if she belonged to the species herself. There's a refrain of a Boz Scaggs song I hear on the radio that always reminds me of Hayat: "Sometimes I cry, sometimes I fly like a bird."

Several years later, after Hayat had died, I told the following story, which I had heard her recount often, at her memorial service. Over the years Hayat had had several friends who claimed to channel spirits from the other side. One woman channeled a spirit named Esme, who loved to speak with Hayat. In one conversation Hayat asked Esme if it were true that we reincarnate into different bodies after death. Esme said that it was. "But how will I know it's *me*?" asked Hayat. "How did you know it was *you* this time?" answered Esme.

Because I was still on disability and because my friends had been so generous in driving me to doctor's appointments, I began to drive Hayat on some of her medical rounds. Unlike most people I knew, she enjoyed riding in my behemoth Oldsmobile, and she approved of the way I didn't interfere in her business.

This became my normal routine. Several times a week I went to physical therapy, had lunch with Hayat, drove her to an appointment, and hung out at the Knitting Basket or went home to work on my red cashmere sweater. It was a pleasant and relaxing time, with plenty of opportunity for spiritual conversation and creative exploration, but of course it was only an interlude and couldn't last. Soon I would have to return to work.

CHAPTER SEVEN

Desperately Seeking

I BEGAN STUDYING IN ARICA, a school of mysticism and meditation, in 1974, because I was desperate at the time to find a way out of drug addiction. I got far more than I'd bargained for. Arica's underlying intellectual theory was and is as compelling as anything I have ever come across, its practices light-years ahead of anything else I've done. I took an almost voluptuous pleasure in the meditations and was fascinated by the breadth and possibilities of the limitless inner world. My journalist's penchant for the inside story was fostered by membership in a mystical school, where nothing was ever the way it appeared, just as it had been encouraged in left-wing politics, where nothing was ever the way people in power said it was. Nonetheless, I had a hard time keeping up with the Arica work, which progressed by levels through vigorous trainings, and often lagged behind my friends and working companions. Still, Arica provided me with the foundation of everything I know about esoteric mysticism.

Though most of my friends in Arica had come to the school after years of spiritual seeking, traveling through Zen Buddhism, transcendental meditation, Gestalt therapy, and virtually every divergent element of the human potential movement of the sixties and seventies, I had come to it because I wanted to stop using drugs. Now, ironically, after five years of recovery from drug addiction, with nearly twenty years' study in Arica, I found myself, for the first time in my life, actively seeking spiritual answers, willing to explore other paths, mysteriously encountering one teacher after another. My need for physical healing had led me on a search for spiritual healing as well.

I kept on going to twelve-step recovery meetings, though often they bored me to tears; I knitted constantly to keep the boredom at bay. "Hey, man," my friend Nancy's husband teased my boyfriend the first time he saw me knitting at a meeting, "I didn't know you were dating Grandma." I needed knitting not only to save my mind from boredom, but also to find my way through the confusing thicket of spiritual options that now appeared to me. It was a haven of peace I could retreat to whenever I became overwhelmed.

In Arica I had enjoyed the practice called "The Nine Ways of Zhikr" more than any other exercise we did. Its devotional aspect and the ecstatic altered state it produced appealed to my nature. Sufi *zikr*, as we performed it with Sheikh Taner Vargonen of the Qadiri-Rifa'i order, who had come to us from Turkey via Kalamazoo, Michigan, started and ended with the bedrock repetition "*La illaha il Allah*," there is no God but God. This was a statement I could live with. The purpose of *zikr*, Taner told us, was to open the heart and annihilate the false self ruled by the ego. *Sufi* comes from the word *suf*, or wool, and refers to wearers of the patched woolen cloaks who stood in the streets with begging bowls as a measure of their humility and their detachment from the material plane.

Zikr is so powerful an exercise that it can change even the chemical composition of the body. In New York I once saw Sheikh Muzaffer of the Helveti-Jerrahi order pierce the cheek of a dervish in *fana*, or mystical ecstasy, with a long skewer. The dervish didn't bleed, and his skin showed no scar after the ceremony. In Taner's *zikr* I experienced many phenomena, on one occasion accumulating so much heat in my hands that I thought I would burn a hole in my pants when I rested my palms on my legs. I also enjoyed my relationship with Taner, who treated me like a sister. He was accessible and down-to-earth; he had once supported himself by delivering pizzas in Kalamazoo. It is often said of Sufis that they are "in the world but not of it"; Taner possessed that precise quality of being.

Perhaps the search I am attempting to describe will sound like a kind of spiritual dilettantism, as I am treating weighty subjects, each one of which could easily fill all the pages of this book, with the briefest possible explanations. My intentions, however, could not have been more sincere. I was looking, at the time, for a way to draw closer to the Creator, in whom I believed with all my heart, for strength, guidance, comfort, and the evolution of my soul, and I was willing to try any number of things to find the way that suited me best. So I stayed in Arica, went to twelve-step meetings, was initiated into the Sufi order, attended sweat lodges and Native American ceremonies with Jimmy, and kept my eyes and ears attuned to still other possibilities. I characterized this period in my life to my friend Karen, who was similarly inclined, as a time of "spiritual overexertion."

I soon found that I was spreading myself much too thin. Each group, each organization, each community had its birthday parties, its potlucks, its holidays, its necessary observances. Jimmy went to a sweat lodge almost every day and became impatient with me when I didn't show the same dedication. Taner's teaching became more rigidly religious, and I grew correspondingly more uneasy.

Also, with my arm more or less healed, it was time for me to return to work rewriting my first book. I no longer had the same leisurely stretches of time to spend with Hayat, since my concentration was destroyed if I took time out to see her in the middle of the day. Gracious friend that she was, she told me she would send me "energy on the inner plane." But she couldn't understand why my writing took so long to finish, and I couldn't really explain it to her.

Gradually and painfully I withdrew from everyone and everything as my work absorbed my attention. It was as though I descended down through layers of consciousness to the place where my writing came from, and as I dove deeper, becoming further submerged, social interaction began to seem more stressful and irrelevant. During one especially intense period of writing, I could not even carry on a conversation with another person. I felt somewhat guilty about my retreat from the groups with which I had been so enthusiastically engaged, but there was nothing I could do about it; I had to do my work.

What I had learned in the *zikrs* and from Hayat dovetailed with the cumulative wisdom of my recovery from addiction. Sufism is a method for purifying and opening the heart, getting in touch with the place where you feel your deepest connection to the Creator. The twelve steps of recovery direct us to pray for knowledge of God's will for us and for the power to carry it out. The only way I could imagine knowing God's will for me was by experiencing it in the pure impulses of my heart, by trusting what I truly wanted and what made me feel happy when I did it. For me that was writing and the many forms of creativity that nourished it; these things had to come first in my life. Now with my work beginning again in earnest, I realized that I had often shortchanged my own creative process. For years I'd been willing to neglect my inner life for a relationship with a man or for drugs or because someone else's needs or theory or work or life seemed somehow more important than mine. But I couldn't do that anymore. The most critical commitment I now had to make was to myself and my writing; everyone and everything else would just have to wait.

Oddly enough, what came to sustain me was knitting. I used my knitting to sink down into the deep creative well that was the source of my writing, and I knitted to rise to the surface when I had finished my work for the day. Since the red heart sweater was my own design, I had to figure complex mathematical calculations, which I scribbled, along with my unanswered telephone messages, on the back of whichever envelope was handy. I could lose myself in the knitting, relax, and think things through when I was stuck, all without becoming distracted from the work at hand. My knitting gave me serenity and demanded nothing of me in return. In addition, it was producing something beautiful and something also uniquely mine.

Due to my particular genetic inheritance, I have narrow shoulders and a wide chest measurement. Every conventional pattern I had ever followed with the set-in sleeves I liked (most patterns today employ an easier dropped shoulder and straight-edged sleeve) either fell off my shoulders if the bust fit or hugged my shoulders and strained at the bust. Working with the most expensive yarn I had ever purchased, I took the biggest risk I had ever chanced and decreased stitches far into the body for the armholes, several inches past the most generous allowance prescribed. As I worked on the red sweater, I sometimes had the feeling that I was being guided by an inner teacher. The bands of pattern themselves had their own logical integrity so that they almost dictated the shaping of the various pieces. I don't know where it came from, but in making this sweater I had a daring I had never possessed, and I was willing to fly by the seat of my pants to make something that matched both my own specifications and my idiosyncratic personal preferences. I like a high neckline; I made the neckline an inch higher than it would normally have been. I copied the sleeves from an old sweater I liked, narrowed them, and fitted them high in the armhole as the French designer Sonia Rykiel used to do. I risked and dared and trusted myself, basing my calculations on a self-knowledge that was also new to me, an honest examination of what I really looked like and what I preferred.

The results were splendid. I was more pleased with how the red sweater fitted me and expressed my vision than I had ever been before. I wore it at those times when I wanted to look especially good. It represented many things to me but none more than that finally, after years of blindly following others, I had begun to trust myself.

Where did this change come from? Was it as sudden and dramatic as it appeared, or was it simply the natural outcome of a patient accumulation of small changes that had occurred slowly over the years? Was it really that momentous? One little sweater, after all, is not that important in the cosmic scheme of things. And compared to the grand traditions I'd been exploring, knitting seemed weighted to their monumental spirituality as a fly to an elephant. Did the change come from the writing? From *zikr*? Did it happen because I'd broken my arm and had to find a new way to think and work? Or did it come from everything I'd done up to now, my new self-knowledge the fruit of hard work and continuing recovery? I had no answers but only more questions and then still more, as time went by and the self-knowledge grew, sometimes out of control.

Some sort of lamp had been lit in my mind, and its light began leaking into other corners of my life as well. One of the fundamental tenets of Judaism is that every single human has a direct relationship with God, one that requires no priest or intermediary. Equally fundamental to the twelve-step programs is every participant's absolute right to a God of his or her own understanding. I don't know if it came from a basic anarchism or perhaps was the product of restlessness and a short attention span, but I began to question the spiritual authority of every outside expert I'd encountered. I had begun with a hunger for contact with the Creator. Now something had shifted, subtly perhaps, but as deeply as a seismic fissure, and I began to think I would have to find my own way alone. A mysterious inner teacher had dictated the shaping of my red heart sweater; were there spiritual guides within me as well? What was the source of the still small voice I'd learned to listen to in recovery?

In Arica we'd been taught, "Everything you need is already inside you." Most spiritual teachers offered a road map to find that knowledge, to remember what you already knew. But I was having difficulty, as I did when driving, in asking anyone else for directions. I began to think that just as I hadn't been able to fit anyone else's garment to my own particular body, I might have to forge a solitary path to fit my peculiar metaphysical being. But because these were spiritual matters, and I have no spiritual authority, I doubted myself endlessly. Had I now reached the heights of grandiosity and folly? Who did I think I was?

During this time of intense questioning, I took a trip to Minnesota and visited my old friend Mike Jones at the hotel he managed "below the safety net," as he called it, where he had caught and rescued me in the depths of my junkie despair.

"I just don't understand it," I told him. "I know all these meditations and exercises. I've studied some of the top spiritual traditions and have been accepted into the practices of other cultures. I know teachers I love and respect. But I can't stick with any of their disciplines. What's wrong with me? Why can't I make a commitment?"

He was silent awhile, and when he spoke it was slowly. "Because none of them is *your* tradition," he said.

CHAPTER EIGHT

Earth Walk

OVER MANY VISITS to my parents in Florida, I had developed the habit of walking forty-five minutes each day. It was a good break from the sedentary business of knitting, compatible with the contemplative rhythms engendered by the work, and there was plenty to see in my parents' neighborhood. In all the places where the Everglades have been drained and the land filled to build houses, canals still run alongside the main streets and roads.

Despite the development, the feeling and atmosphere of swampland pervade the area and crop up in sometimes surprising ways. The black water canals are home to large fish and snapping turtles; they lure raccoons and waterbirds to their banks to fish and at times disgorge odd creatures like the family of poisonous toads that liked to hang out around my parents' garage. On my walks around the canals I glimpsed a flock of green parrots that had grown from a runaway pair as well as cardinals, with a tropical richness to their red plumage, kingfishers, and my favorite neighbors, a family of tiny burrowing owls that nested on the ground of a nearby yard.

I emerged from these walks strengthened and refreshed and decided to continue them when I returned to California. In my ideal world, I'd be walking along the ocean every day, but I live too far away and so had to content myself with a stretch of San Francisco Bay shoreline along the coast of Alameda, a peninsula in the East Bay.

At the time I began walking, I was troubled by my inability to engage in a regular spiritual practice or to commit to a specific path. It occurred to me that as I could find nothing that suited my needs, I might have to work out something of my own, and, as it happened, this grew out of the discoveries I made as a knitter and from my walks along the shore.

I walked to clear my mind, to build strength and stamina in my body, and to develop a closer relationship with myself, my higher power, and the physical world of nature. I used my walking time to observe the landscape around me and also to practice my prayer and meditation for the day. If my life were exactly the way I wanted, I would start the morning with some meditation, go for a long walk, come home to do a good day's writing, and knit for hours in the evening after a nice dinner I cooked myself. In reality, I'm lucky if I manage to do even one or two of those things in a day.

Normally I walked about three miles. My route was always the same. I began at Crab Cove Park, between the twin royal palms, and made my way along the edge of the grassy knolls, through the big windblown cypress trees, past the smelly duck pond, around the meadows near the tree where the hummingbirds nested, past the picnic grounds and stands of pampas grass, and finally onto the straightaway, the long stretch of beach that runs for miles, all the way to Bay Farm Island.

Sometimes I prayed while I walked; other times I moved my feet to a silent rhythm I heard inside my head. On many days I laboriously made my way through the tangle of psychic rubbish that tumbled out of my mind. And always I looked around. The attention to detail I had

had to cultivate as a knitter now served me well in observing my surroundings. Each walk seemed to contain a surprise. One day a kestrel lighted on a pole in front of me; on another I watched pelicans fishing, skimming closely over the water, then dive-bombing for fish. I noticed when and where the wildflowers bloomed; I observed which way the seeds blew and how the colors blended from one strain to another as they spread. I noted the varied shades of green of the different grasses and the seasons in which the Canadian geese stopped in the park and the red-winged blackbirds migrated through.

Views from the shoreline constantly changed. Mornings were foggy; hot days brought a disheartening line of brown smog along the hills. At times San Francisco, across the bay, emerged from the mist like the fabled land of Avalon. Everything vanished and reappeared like magic according to the whims of the fog. Some days water and air merged in a single shade of silvery gray; others every detail stood out in stark, vivid relief. I walked through everything: rain, fog, sweltering heat, and wind so strong that the normally placid bay rose up in waves that slapped along the shore.

My prayers and meditations were an odd mix of things I had learned in Arica, from Judaism, in Native American sweat lodges, from Sufi group, and from practices that I had read of among Buddhists and heard about in twelve-step meetings. Every day they were the same and also different. Mainly what I tried to do was listen and be attentive to what was going on around me, to watch how it changed through the four seasons, as I continued to walk over time.

Just as knitting had given me a way to sit still without boredom, sitting still had slowed me down and deepened my thought processes; it had rendered me capable of a kind of one-pointed concentration I now applied to the outer world. I wanted to deeply know that piece of ground I walked on and, in learning it, to sink deeper into myself. In the end I found what I was looking for there: I learned to listen for the heartbeat of Mother Earth and to try to move in harmony with her rhythms, to "walk in beauty," as the Navajos say.

I've learned invaluable things from my spiritual teachers and will always be grateful for everything they've taught me, but I had simply reached a point where I had to strike out on my own.

I began to follow my own heart and inner guidance wherever they might lead. Setting out on my earth walk, I consulted only one book, the one Hayat had recommended I study: "the sacred manuscript of nature."

CHAPTER NINE

God and Nature, Nature and Cloth

WHEN HAYAT HAD READ to me from the writings of Hazrat Inayat Khan, her beloved "Murshid," who founded the Sufi Order of the West, she had begun with the Ten Sufi Thoughts, one of which commanded my absolute attention. "There is one holy book, the sacred manuscript of nature, the only scripture which can enlighten the reader," it read.

The statement resonated with what I felt inside. When I thought about what I'd like to know, what I would consider a genuine level of spiritual attainment for myself, I discovered that I wished to have a deeper and more empathetic understanding of the mysteries of nature.

My friend David Getz, who has worked as both a visual artist and a drummer, says that nature is full of rhythm and repetition and that even people who are not artists express their response to nature with pattern. From the first rhythm we hear, our mother's heartbeat, we expand our awareness and comprehension of the world around us, and we seek to duplicate its beauty and fathom its secrets by depicting it in symbols and patterns. For example, the frequently used patterns of pioneer quilt makers expressed what they saw in their world: flying geese, tumbling blocks, double wedding rings, Virginia reels, as well as the stories and myths that lent mystery to their lives, such as the story of Jacob's ladder. In the intricate knitting combinations used in Aran sweaters, the names of the stitches tell a story of the knitters' world: marriage lines (up and down), honeycomb, blackberry vines, ocean waves, tree of life, and so forth.

Somehow, though I have no quarrel with fine art, what has spoken to me aesthetically throughout my life is the handwork of indigenous peoples who live close to nature. I have been unimaginably moved by the almost primeval human desire to make sense out of the un-

knowable and to fashion beauty out of the ordinary objects of everyday life.

Recently I read a story in the newspaper about a pho-
tographer who went around the world celebrating the
work of women in various cultures. In Guatemala she
asked Lucia Sicay Choguaj, a mother of three, what ac-
complishment she felt proudest of. The skilled artisan
displayed her exquisite weaving. "Anyone can have children," she said. Guatemalans seem to be an entire nation
of artists. The riotous colors of their public gathering
places and the patterns of their clothing are a feast for the
eyes, each length of woven *ikat* cotton more beautiful
than the last. But what is even more remarkable about
the cloth the Guatemalan women weave on backstrap
looms from earliest childhood is that it has preserved
whole the Mayan culture from which these women de-
scend.

When the Spanish conquistadores first encountered
the native peoples of South and Central America, they
gained such easy access to the stores of gold partly because what the Incas valued most highly was not their
gold but their woven cloth. Their best cloth was woven
for the sun. Cloth. What could be more ordinary and
thus more sacred than the making and wearing of fabric
to clothe the human body? As Lenore Tawney, a weaver

who is legendary among her peers, says, "We wear fiber and are closer to fiber than almost anything else. It's our diapers—and our shrouds."

No matter what else was going on in Mahatma Gandhi's life, he chose to spin without ceasing. Why did he spin? To keep himself closely tied to the earth and to ordinary people? Because the simple repetitive rhythm helped him to think and cope with the stresses of his life? I don't know but can only extrapolate from my own and others' experience. In a recent study commissioned by the American Home Sewing & Craft Association, New York University researchers gave subjects simple sewing projects and fitted them with blood pressure monitor cuffs and fingertip electrodes. On the average, heart rate dropped eight beats per minute for beginners and eleven for experienced sewers. This goes with the "forget therapy; just knit" school of stress reduction, and it also mimics some of the better known physiological effects of meditation.

How might we explain this? For one thing, cloth is basic to human life. We are meant to wear clothing we create ourselves to protect us from the elements. The self-expression that shows in how we decorate our clothing and tells what we have to say about ourselves and our world is an added bonus. In this area, particularly, I've always best understood the Mies van der Rohe quote,

"God is in the details." A crudely made garment may be every bit as functional and utilitarian as a finely made one, but the piece made with pride in quality, refined aesthetic judgment, and well-developed craftsmanship transcends the utilitarian purpose it was created to serve and elevates the being of its maker.

If we are indeed made in the image of our Creator, it stands to reason that we are most like that Creator when we are creating something ourselves. So the very act is sacred, from the most humble piecing of fabric for a patchwork quilt to the soaring stonework of the great Gothic cathedrals. The desire to make things to wear, to use as tools, and to record how we live and what we see in our lives is probably hardwired into the human psyche. Taste and aesthetic judgment are functions of intuition; we believe something to be beautiful even when we may not be able to explain just why it pleases us. Yet we are driven with all the power we possess to create beauty, and the hunger of our souls when we lack a means of creative expression is almost palpable. Furthermore, the making of cloth or other objects we need for everyday life lends itself naturally to ritual, and ritual also is basic to human life.

I've always loved the saying *Laborare et orare*, work is prayer. From a Marxist perspective, work that you are alienated from—on an assembly line, for instance, repetitively fashioning a part of a product you will not own or use for the enrichment of a person you may never know—is as different from handknitting as Brazil is from Antarctica. Consider a grandmother knitting a sweater for a grandchild just coming into the world. Into the stitches of that sweater go all the grandmother's prayers for a safe delivery, all of her good feelings about the child and its parents. The work itself is a prayer for the safety and well-being of mother and child, a labor of love, a ritual welcoming of new life inside the extended family or tribe.

If this is a romantic view of life, so be it. My spiritual ancestors may well be the proponents of the arts and crafts movement, whose furniture, architecture, and aesthetic philosophy have enriched my own area of northern California. The wildly imaginative architects Bernard Maybeck and Julia Morgan helped turn Berkeley into a garden of earthly delights. I also think of the Shakers, who managed to express their views of God and humankind in the simplest aspects of everything they made. When I used to own and collect quilts, what appealed to me was the life and the history they contained, the souls of the women who had stitched them, the shadow of the maker that remains behind in the objects that come from her or his hands.

It used to drive me crazy when I made mistakes in my knitting. I wanted things to come out perfect, whatever that means, and was disappointed when they didn't. Years ago someone, I can't recall who, told me that weavers of Persian carpets always intentionally include a mistake in their carefully constructed designs "because only Allah is perfect." Once I knew that, I could more easily accept my own mistakes, and I began to look for these intentional imperfections in other objects I came across.

The Huichol Indians, descendants of the Aztecs, who live in the mountains of Mexico in the state of Nayarit, have maintained their traditional art, culture, and spiritual way of life since pre-Columbian times. They have a long tradition of shamanism and ritual peyote use, and they carry their peyote in cross-stitch-embroidered shoulder bags. Elliot Cowan, author of the book *Plant Spirit Medicine,* who is apprenticed to a Huichol medicine man, told me that the women who do the embroidery must undergo a lengthy shamanic training in which they ask the Creator to give them the visions to depict in their work. Their embroidery, then, serves as a measure of their spiritual attainment.

All traditional Huichol clothing is colorful and elaborately embroidered, and the Huichol vision of life and spirit is expressed in their better-known crafts of yarn painting and masks and bowls in which seed beads have been laboriously embedded one by one in a base of beeswax to form a picture. Yet the designs of the cross-stitched shoulder bags are simple and geometric. A distinctive feature of their geometry, however, is that the symmetry is deliberately broken.

This imperfection, as in the spirit path of Navajo weavings, denotes the spiritual aspect of the design. In many indigenous cultures with highly developed craft techniques, the finest objects may be reserved for ritual or ceremonial use. For example, the Pomo Indians of northern California are famous for their intricately woven feather baskets. In the best baskets, made for ceremony, one part of the basket is left deliberately unfeathered. "The unfeathered part," writes Susan Billy, a basket weaver and curator of the Pomo exhibit at the National Museum of the American Indian in New York,

> may be the *dau*, an intentional irregularity in the design. The dau prevents bad feelings or spirits from being trapped in the basket, and it also allows good feelings and spirits to enter and fill the basket. It's the spirit door that allows spirits to move freely within the basket.

Almost halfway across the continent, the master potters of the Southwestern pueblos employ a similar effect. In *The American Indian Craft Book*, Marz and Nono Minor write,

The gap in encircling lines on jars or bowls, commonly
known as the "exit trail of life," "ceremonial path," or "spirit
path," is constantly used in Santo Domingo decoration.
The ancient belief persists that every pot is the abiding
place of a spirit which is manifested by the resonance of the
vessel when tapped, and that to curb its freedom of exit and
return by painting completely encircling lines is to endan-
ger the vessel which may be broken through the efforts of
the spirit to pass these barriers. Breaks in lines occur in
more than 90 percent of all Santo Domingo pottery.

There is another, unseen dimension to the making of
objects, and its mystical importance stems directly and
precisely from its absence. The tai chi teacher, a character in Lynne Sharon Schwartz's novel, *The Fatigue Artist*,
speaks eloquently to this subject:

> "Chinese art did make beautiful things, poems, paintings,
> pottery, all with a great deal of empty space. The empty
> space represents the inner life, what is most important but
> unseen. Like the breath, which is invisible but sustains us
> . . . The space in a bowl, for instance . . . You use the clay
> to make it, and that is the part you see, but what makes the
> bowl useful is the space within. That metaphor is from
> Lao-tzu, to give proper credit."

When I began to knit something, I wasn't thinking of
its spiritual purpose or of the empty space within that

would make the sweater useful. Nor did I need to place imperfections in my knitting deliberately, as they occurred on a regular basis despite my best efforts to avoid them. If I knitted something with a complicated pattern, where I constantly had to be counting rows and stitches, I often made a mistake the moment my mind began to wander. Sometimes I would rip out enough rows to correct the problem, sometimes not, but I began to appreciate these mistakes as small lessons in mindfulness or humility and as expressions of the spirit or soul of the knitting, which seemed to exist apart from me, the knitter. My experience of knitting was enriched the more I knew of spiritual matters, and vice versa. And I found that once I could accept my lack of perfection in both areas with humor and grace, the whole business of knitting, as well as of living, became far more pleasurable to me.

I cannot raise the issue of perfection here without being reminded of a Nasrudin story I originally heard in Sheikh Taner's group. The Mulla Nasrudin is a stock character who appears in many Sufi teaching tales. To the Sufi, intention is everything, purity of heart more important than rigid adherence to form. And this is the story that proves it. It seems the Mulla Nasrudin was crossing over a bridge when he heard the sounds of *zikr* coming from an island in the river below. Much to his dismay, a dervish on the island was performing *zikr* improperly. Nasrudin hastened to the riverbank, where he engaged a boatman to take him to the island, and there he proceeded to admonish and correct the dervish. The dervish humbly thanked him for his help, and Nasrudin instructed the boatman to return him to shore. They had not gone more than halfway across the river when Nasrudin was astonished to see the dervish running along on top of the water, chasing after the boat and calling out to him, "Mulla, Mulla, you forgot to tell me the right way to breathe."

Weaving is among the most ancient and almost mythological of crafts. Who can forget the image of the Fates weaving their elaborate tapestry, deciding the destiny or lifespan of this or that human, ending a life with the simple snip of a thread? The spider, or arachnid, is named for the mythical character Arachne, who challenged the goddess Diana to a weaving contest (never a good idea). Arachne is supposed to have led her lover out of the labyrinth of the minotaur with a single silken thread but was unfortunately turned into a spider when Diana was thrown into a fit of pique by the results of the weaving contest.

A woman weaving may create the universe. Nancy Rosoff at the National Museum of the American Indian writes about the Huichols, "Through the process of weaving, a woman achieves a deeper understanding of her physical, social and spiritual world. The textile, therefore, is a symbolic re-creation of this knowledge."

The technique of weaving called *ikat* employs a tied and dyed warp. When the weft is woven across it, designs such as animals or people may appear. You have probably seen this sort of weaving in Guatemalan, Japanese, or Indonesian textiles. There is a cloth, however, called the Balinese *geringseng*, which is made with a double *ikat*, tied and dyed across both warp and weft, an almost impossibly difficult technique to imagine. The *geringseng* is considered a magical object, an heirloom treasured and passed down in families, and is used to protect women in childbirth or elders on their deathbeds. Every aspect of the making of a *geringseng* is completely ritualized, from beginning to end, and it may require as long as nine years to complete one. A friend of mine who collects Indonesian textiles says, "With the double *ikat*, images emerge from the fabric almost like ghosts."

Magical cloth. Many proscriptions and superstitions govern the making of handcrafted garments. In the knitting of Scottish fishing gansies, for instance, the yarn was to be dyed with only certain colors. Although lichens or mosses growing on the rocks produced desirable colors, these would never be used for dyeing, says Norman

Kennedy, a traditional Scottish folksinger and craftsperson, "because what comes from the rocks goes to the
rocks." When dealing with so potentially powerful an ad-
versary as the sea, one couldn't use enough magic to protect a sailor. It is nowadays commonly thought that the
ivory wool Aran sweaters were each made in distinctive
patterns so that a drowned sailor could be identified by
his sweater. Norman Kennedy doesn't believe this is so
because the Aran design is so comparatively recent a part
of Irish history. However, as he says, "It's folklore, and
folklore is made every day."

As with weaving, handknitting lends to a garment an almost totemic quality that derives from its closeness to nature. If the garment is made of wool, the fleece came
from living sheep, and often the burrs and brambles the
sheep wandered through must be disentangled from
the yarn. As a knitter works, her hair may become bound
up in the stitches—this has happened in every sweater I
ever made—and certainly it marks the garment in almost
a pagan magical way. Even in the twentieth century we
hope to protect our loved ones from perilous circum-
stances beyond our control, and we may resort to the
myths and superstitions of ancient times to do so, literally
"weaving a spell," as the oldtime Scottish women cast

their spells with red yarn wound in a pattern on the ground.

Knitting as a technique may well have originated in ancient Egypt. Thanks to moths, precious little has remained of historical knitting, but we can surmise that as the human body has remained unchanged through the centuries, knitting was required to cover body parts, such as the feet, that needed close-fitting yet flexible fabric. To jump around in history a bit, the American Red Cross formed as a ladies' auxiliary during the Civil War to knit socks for the soldiers of the Union Army. As many an army has discovered through time, a soldier is only as good as the condition of his feet, and these in turn may be only as good as the quality of his socks.

The Shetland Islanders, at the tip of Scotland, raised sheep whose fleece was particularly light and fluffy. Though remote seeming, the islands actually were located along major shipping routes, and the islanders made a living through the centuries knitting socks and underwear for traveling sailors. Shetland Islanders were renowned for being able to spin their fleece so fine that a whole shawl could be knitted and fit through a wedding ring. These shawls often took a year to knit and were so costly they could be afforded only by the nobility. According to Alice Starmore, the Fair Isle designer, when knitting machines were invented and began producing the goods the islanders had relied on to put food on their tables, they were forced to come up with another product with commercial value, and that's how the distinctive colored style evolved, reaching its high point of popularity in the 1920s, when the Prince of Wales was photographed wearing a Fair Isle vest for golf.

Any craftsperson, when setting out to make something, connects to a heritage so ancient and broad based that it makes the mind reel. Handcrafts connect one to the physical world and to the spiritual worlds as well. Like the "lovely hula hands" of the sacred Hawaiian dancer, the hands of knitters and craftspeople spin tales of creation, life, death, genealogy, and history; they connect us to the heavens, the ages, and the earth itself at once. To knit is to be freed from time and the constraints of everyday life, to take our place at the table of the ancients, to claim citizenship of the entire planetary culture and relationship with the widest community of people from the present and the past. The humble knitter sits in the center between heaven and earth. As she spins the yarn to make her sacred cloth, invisible threads connect her to both God and Mother Earth.

CHAPTER TEN

Dreaming of Dragons

I PROMISED MYSELF THAT WHEN I finished my book I would embark on a sweater project so complex and intricate that it could absorb my total attention. I'd had my eye on something in the Annabel Fox book for quite a while: a swirling pattern of entwined dragons in blues, reds, and ivories on a dark blue ground. The design had been inspired by a Ming vase. Making it involved a kind of color work I had never done before, which looked about as difficult as it's possible for knitting to get. I was somewhat daunted by the prospect of trying it, but the thought of learning something new intrigued me, and I liked the bare bones of the sweater, its lines.

The technique of knitting a picture into fabric is called intarsia. Fair Isle knitting also creates pictures, but its defining quality is that only two colors are used in any given row. With intarsia knitting, each row may contain as many colors as the pattern requires, sometimes quite a large number. I had knitted Fair Isle yokes before but had never attempted anything so complicated as these dragons. When I tried to prepare for it by knitting a multicolored sample swatch, I spent an entire Saturday tangled in yarn, getting nowhere at all. By the end of that day I was so bound up in frustration that with any sense I would have quit right there, but of course I didn't.

Instead I went to the Knitting Basket for help. Sheila, one of the women who works there, who comes from England ("with Irish tendencies," as she says) and has been knitting since childhood, showed me a method for doing color work. Normally I knit Continental style, which means you pick the yarn off the index finger of your left hand, which acts as a shuttle, by moving the needle with your right hand. In American-style knitting, you manually place the yarn around the needle by "throwing" it with your right hand. Sheila told me that in order to do color work I would have to knit both ways simultaneously, alternating Continental style with my left hand and American style with my right. If this sounds impossibly confusing, imagine how difficult it is to do. The degree of manual dexterity it required boggled my mind; I was in despair of ever being able to learn it. Even after a lifetime of knitting, when I tried to combine the two styles, my fingers felt as stiff and awkward as a beginner's, and I lapsed into utter incompetence.

Still, I am nothing if not tenacious once an obsession has taken root in my mind, and I had fallen in love with a Chinese lacquer red chenille that featured prominently in the pattern. So I went home and practiced. I managed to master at least part of the technique (the other part, for carrying extra yarn neatly behind the work, I still haven't learned to do). Then I decided to start my sweater with a sleeve, which had only a single dragon and looked far easier than the body.

The pattern had been drawn out on graph paper with a series of different typographical symbols (open squares, closed squares, circles, and so on) to denote the various colors. I had to enlarge the pattern and fill in the squares with colored pencils before I could even begin to understand what I was supposed to do. Then I had to keep track of what row I was on by having the graph paper spread out before me at all times, weighted down on the sides, with a ruler resting just below the row I was currently working.

One of my favorite things about knitting is the establishing of a rhythm that carries through the work. Rhythm is paramount in producing the psychic serenity that usually accompanies knitting. Just as a shaman will ride a drumbeat out of his body and into the spirit world, a knitter will trail the soothing rhythm of the clicking needles into the deep quiet recesses of her mind.

With the dragon sweater, it was impossible to establish a rhythm, and the work proceeded with such agonizing slowness that I thought I would lose my mind. I could have knit a whole other sweater, with twining cables and twenty different stitch panels, in the time it took me to complete one sleeve. Any given row required between twelve and twenty colors. No sooner had I gone a few stitches with one or two than I had to put them down and pick up new colors, consulting each square of the graphed-out pattern at every turn. Mind you, in knitting one cannot just pick up a color and put it in as would be done in a painting. Each new yarn has to be anchored into the fabric, and the other colors must be carried along the back, loosely enough that they allow the fabric to stretch yet not so loosely that they gap. Attach, knit, strand, twist, carry, stretch the stitches, weave in the thread. And to make matters worse, the balls of colored yarn constantly became entangled and would have to be unwound.

The work was so difficult that I had to talk out loud to myself in order to keep track of the procedure. "Light blue here; strand the red across the back; anchor the red; okay now, pick up the dark blue for two stitches." I felt like a crazy person. I was concentrating so hard to be able to do it that when I put the work down, I could almost feel my mind spring back outward, as though it had been compressed by a giant rubber band. In Arica, Oscar Ichazo had taught us a series of exercises called Kinerhythms, somewhat akin to rubbing your stomach in a counterclockwise motion while patting the top of your head, only more complex and requiring more intense focus. He said that these exercises, when mastered, would "make the brain sing." That's how I felt about the dragon sweater. Only it wasn't making my brain sing; it was making it groan in anguish.

After a weekend of struggling with the sleeve, I went back to the Knitting Basket on Monday. This time Linda showed me how to cut lengths of yarn for each color so that the strings trailed off the bottom of the row and were far easier to untangle than balls of yarn or bobbins. Two indispensable tips had now been provided to me by the knitting ladies to ease this difficult project, yet each time I worked on it my head still felt like it was going to explode.

In Chinese culture the dragon is a powerful totem. It symbolizes heaven, the ethereal realms of the spirit. The dragon chases the pearl of wisdom in an eternal quest for enlightenment. In ancient times only royal figures were permitted to wear the dragon on their clothing, as it was thought to bestow upon the wearer the power of heaven. It's interesting that the Chinese chose a mythological creature to symbolize the spiritual realms, as both are unseen and therefore must be imagined. A willingness to believe in what cannot be seen is a cornerstone of the spiritual life. We may take on faith or grasp by intuition the existence of that which we cannot see; either way a belief in it stands firmly at odds with the empirical scientific view of the Western mind-set.

In Western mythology dragons were more often seen as symbols of fear or superstition. Ancient maps faded out at the edges of the known world with the legend "Here there be dragons." In Christianity St. George slew the dragon and vanquished the forces of ignorance. So one might say that Europeans viewed the imaginative and mythological world as inferior knowledge from the past that had been supplanted by superior wisdom culled from scientific exploration and experimentation. Eastern philosophy, on the other hand, saw in this imaginative world the possibility for expanding the limited horizons of the physical plane into infinite areas of transcendental knowledge. Of course, of the two, I vastly preferred the Eastern view. I wanted the pearl without price, the one the dragon chased through the heavens.

The quest for enlightenment leads into the interior; it is a matter of charting the unknown reaches of the inner world instead of believing that the outer world—what you can see and touch with your senses—is all there is. As one Native American teacher, Blackwolf Jones, puts it, the quest for enlightenment is "the path that leads to the center of your being." The path is internal and filled with the inexplicable and the unexpected. Buddhists know that one can never understand the full dimensions of reality with just the rational mind. That is the purpose of the Zen koan, an unanswerable question such as "What is the sound of one hand clapping?" With the koan the teacher shocks the student's mind into an awareness of its own absurdity. Only when the student is able to admit the possibility that she may not know what she thought she did does real learning become possible.

∞

As I worked on this almost impossibly difficult sweater in a fever of intense concentration, I seemed to become inhabited by dragons. I began to see them everywhere, and they even surfaced in my dreams. Suddenly I noticed dragons twining around elaborately tattooed arms. I recalled dragon references in drug lingo: addicts who smoked Persian heroin by melting it on tinfoil and drawing off the smoke with a tube called it "chasing the dragon"; others called opium "dragon seed." I remembered my daughter in high school playing "Dungeons and Dragons," and I recalled the long bedtime story she and an ex-boyfriend of mine had concocted together, "The Story of Marbel and Bellina," which featured a friendly dragon not unlike the famous Puff. Chinese vases in shop windows I passed suddenly jumped into my field of vision, and I paused to admire carvings in ivory and jade. The front panel of my sweater was anchored by a dragon that moved horizontally by curling its body up and down in ridges like a black mamba snake. At night while I slept, this dragon came alive and lumbered across the landscape of my dreams.

Making the sweater was unlike any knitting I had experienced before. It was more like weaving a picture or accumulating the tiny stitches of petit point into a painted impressionist effect. I wrestled with colossal effort every time I sat down to work. When I brought the sweater to Florida to work on at my parents' house, my mother was so flabbergasted she was speechless. She didn't have to speak, however, because I knew what she was thinking, and the same thing was on my mind. Why was I doing this? What was the point? The work was excruciating; a full day's knitting would sometimes produce only one inch of sweater. Yet the dragons steadily grew. One progressed in its funny up-and-down motion; another whipped across the sky. I made myself keep working no matter how I felt: my back hurt, my neck hurt, my eyes hurt, my brain hurt. Unless one had done it oneself, I found myself thinking, no one could possibly imagine what heroics could go into a piece of knitting.

But I knew why I was doing it and why I couldn't give up. I had determined to become a master knitter, which meant I would have to acquire competence in many types of knitting. More important than the technical skills, however, I would have to achieve self-mastery, mastery over myself. In the martial arts, one studies fighting techniques to defeat the enemy within, by building character and developing integrity, discipline, judgment, balance, restraint, and other valued inner attributes. Tai chi, for example, also known as Supreme Ultimate Boxing, is a spiritual as well as a physical discipline, rooted in principles as much as in movement. Though I hadn't known it when I started the sweater, I had embarked on a sort of internal training. And though the work was sometimes torturous, I had to see it through to the end.

I know for a fact that the quality of my work on the dragon sweater is crude and amateurish. Different knitters favor different types of knitting, and someone practiced in color work and intarsia would have done a far better job. But although I love the sweater, despite or perhaps because of the difficulty of its execution, the finished product seems almost beside the point. The purpose of making the sweater seemed rather in being willing to learn something new, no matter how awkward it felt, and to follow wherever it took me. The point was to open my mind to the presence of dragons in symbology, in design, in language, in myths, in my dreams. The importance of doing it was in achieving self-mastery, forging the discipline to keep on working even when it was hard. And the funny thing about that last part is that self-mastery is precisely the quality that will eventually lead you to the heavenly realms, the ones where dragons play.

Don't let me overdo it on the heroism here, though, because once I had sweated and groaned through the front of the sweater and both the sleeves, there was simply no power on heaven or earth strong enough to make me go through that again. Linda and I worked out a compromise where I would knit only one dragon on the back of the sweater, the undulating bottom fellow, and do the rest in solid blue. What a relief! The sweater might still be sitting unfinished in my knitting bag even now if we hadn't decided on that shortcut. One thing I learned while making that sweater is that intricate intarsia color work, though I love its finished results, is simply not for me. Two beautiful Annabel Fox projects currently languish unfinished in my house, and God knows when I'll have the strength to try them again.

The actual knitting benefit I received from the dragon sweater turned out to be entirely unexpected, not at all what I had set out to accomplish. I didn't even realize what it was until after several years had passed. What I'd actually learned was fluency with the two-handed color technique of switching between Continental- and American-style knitting. When it came time to apply it to something I truly loved, traditional Fair Isle knitting, the technique no longer felt awkward and strange. I had done so much of it that by now it came naturally to me; I could switch back and forth at will between the two styles because my hands remembered what they had done. I'd received a sort of initiation by ordeal and had managed to walk off with the prize, the pearl of wisdom, if you will. I was now a practiced two-handed knitter, firmly imbued with the ambidextrous magic, a gift from Sheila, my own hard work, and the dragons who had lumbered through my dreams.

CHAPTER ELEVEN

A Secret Weapon

IN AUGUST OF 1994 I was diagnosed with cancer. I was already having the month from hell before it happened, and of course that didn't help. At the beginning of the month my daughter moved across the country to New York, which was emotionally devastating, both in the anticipation of losing her and in the actual fact of her absence.

Since early April I had been working as a counselor at the Native American treatment center. I had taken the job partly because I wanted the medical benefits—

membership in the giant HMO Kaiser Permanente—but I never dreamed I would need them so badly or so soon.

Ironically, it was because my job required it that I had gone for a physical exam. I had felt a pain in my right side for some time, which I thought might be gall bladder trouble, and when I mentioned it to the nurse practitioner who was my primary care provider, she scheduled me for an ultrasound. Several days after the ultrasound I got a call from her office informing me that they had "found something" and needed to talk to me right away. What they had found was "a small mass" in the area of my left kidney. She urged me to take this extremely seriously and to go for a CT scan as soon as I could.

Sometime before the medical tests began, on a sweltering day near the middle of August, I happened to stop by the Knitting Basket. The carpeted floor was covered with bags of fine Shetland wool in some of the most unusual heathery colors I had ever seen. A shipment had just arrived from Broad Bay, the company that produces Alice Starmore's palette of yarns. Alice Starmore is the knitwear designer best known for bringing traditional Fair Isle knitting into the present and for exporting its techniques to America. She often takes her inspiration from nature and the motifs of her Celtic heritage, but the designs are uniquely hers. I had been looking through one of her books and playing with the idea of making one of her sweaters for several weeks, but when I saw the actual yarns, in close to twenty dazzling shades of green alone, I had to have the materials to begin the project that very day.

The hallmark of Fair Isle knitting is that you never work with more than two colors in any given row, but the patterns are intricate and the needles small. A Fair Isle sweater is usually made on circular needles in one piece with a *steek*, or bridge, knit across any openings. The steek is later cut (that's right, cut) and sewn down. I would get plenty of practice with my newly mastered technique of alternating Continental knitting with my left hand and American with my right hand. But if I had not previously seen Norman Kennedy, the traditional Scottish folk-singer and craftsman, knitting his Fair Isle and had not inspected his steeks myself, I doubt I would have had the courage to try it.

Let me say here, in case you are not a knitter, that just the idea of cutting a piece of handknitting with a pair of scissors causes the average knitter to gasp with horror. As my friend Sue's mother said when I told her what I was doing, "It would take me a very long time to close those scissors." Because I was the first, among all the Knitting Basket's customers or staff, to attempt an Alice Starmore design, I was quickly designated steek pioneer; they would wait to see what happened to my sweater when I cut it before they tried it themselves.

I chose a vest in a design called Oregon, with large pastel leaves on the bottom and stylized evergreen trees repeating on the body. Both the background and foreground colors would be changing in subtle gradations throughout the knitting of the design. This is an Alice Starmore signature and produces a spectacular effect. Though it was well over ninety degrees that day and the thought of wearing a wool sweater couldn't have been further from anyone's mind—the Knitting Basket was virtually deserted—I gathered up my materials in a fever of excitement, went home to start the project, and immediately became obsessed.

My CT scan was scheduled for the third week of the month. With a few days' break from work, I went to stay with my friend Lou and her family at a cabin they had rented on the Russian River. The landscape was strikingly similar to the design of my sweater, hillsides of towering evergreens, redwood, pine, and spruce, with a blue-green river snaking through the canyon. By now I was well into my knitting, and I enjoyed its pictorial reflection of the scenery at hand. I was worried about the CT scan and grateful I had the knitting to provide me with relief and relaxation.

I knew that the techs had seen something abnormal on my CT scan before I was even out of my gown. First they sent me back into the machine for another set of pictures. Then the head of radiology herself took me by the hand and dragged me down the hall for another round of ultrasound. "You're really lucky we found this by accident," she said. "Depends on your definition of luck," I thought to myself. Later in the day my nurse practitioner called on the phone and had me stay on the line while she rang through to the urology department, who set me up with an appointment for Monday. That was Friday afternoon.

Monday morning I went for my appointment. Lou couldn't go with me because her husband was at work and there was no one to baby-sit their son. I still wasn't expecting the worst, so it was a bit of a shock, to say the least, when the urologist put my X rays up on the light board and announced, "You have cancer." Just the sound of that word *cancer* sent alarm bells clanging through every cell of my body.

"How can you be so sure?" I started. "Couldn't it just be a benign cyst?"

"It's cancer," the doctor stated, with so much certainty that even the idea of getting a second opinion flew out the window. I was stunned, in a daze so profound it amounted to an altered state of consciousness, and I struggled to pay attention to the rest of what the doctor was telling me.

He thought it was contained; if so, the prognosis was good, an 85 percent survival rate. The kidney would have to be removed. The only treatment for this type of cancer was surgery; radiation and chemotherapy didn't work on it. His schedule was open, he said, and he could do the surgery on Thursday. "Now go have some lunch," he told me, "and when you come back we'll make the arrangements for surgery."

I called Lou from the pay phone in the lobby. "It's cancer," I said.

"Oh, my God," she said.

We couldn't really say much after that.

I went outside and, in some sort of ambulatory fog, made my way to the pizza joint on the next block. "So I have cancer," I thought to myself, "and now I'm having pizza." I may have been dying, but I still was hungry for lunch.

In the weeks to come I would be surprised by how much those ordinary things combined to keep me sane. All the mundane tasks that normally irritated me — putting gas in the car, washing dishes, writing out bills — kept me grounded in reality and involved in my life, so that no matter how much I may have wanted to curl up in a fetal ball and obsess about the cancer, I still had to take care of business and carry on as best I could. A line of Alfred Kazin's, in an account of a Friday-morning visit to his radiologist's office that I had read in the *New Yorker*, described this feeling perfectly: "In the midst of death we are in life," it read, "and itching to get away for the weekend."

I had been planning to go on vacation with my friend Judy to Lake Vermilion in northern Minnesota and to Bear Butte and some other places in South Dakota. My ticket was bought and paid for, my vacation time scheduled from work. I had been under so much emotional stress at my job that I didn't want to go straight into surgery in that condition. I asked the doctor if two or three weeks would make any difference; I wanted to prepare myself spiritually for what was to come. I didn't know if I would emerge from surgery to find I was dying or that the cancer had spread and I was facing a year of radiation and chemotherapy. He said there was some risk but it was small. I decided to take the risk and scheduled my surgery for three weeks away. Then I staggered out of his office, still in shock.

When I pushed through the double doors to the waiting room, I saw Lou at the reception desk, frantic, looking for me. Her husband had come home from work so that she could be with me at the hospital, a kindness I will always remember. We fell into each other's arms and began sobbing. Other people waiting there turned away or changed seats to give us some privacy. We sobbed and sobbed until our emotions were spent. Then we went out into the glaringly bright day to figure out what to do next.

In memory, the whole rest of that afternoon has the shimmering heightened quality of hallucinogenic experience. Lou and I drove around in her car doing silly things, and by the time a few hours had passed, we were making jokes about cancer. A survival mechanism had kicked in, and far from being flip or cruelly inappropriate, it seemed like a fine and merciful way to cope.

Over the next few days, as I struggled to assimilate the news and to break it to other friends and family members, two things came to me. *First You Cry*, the title of Betty Rollins's memoir of her bout with breast cancer, was much in my mind and best described what was happening to me; I frequently broke down in my car or sitting at my kitchen table or while talking with a friend. And a line from Louise Erdrich's *Love Medicine*, spoken by the character Lulu Lamartine, expressed my deepest inner feelings: "I was in love with the whole world and all that lived in its rainy arms."

I was surprised to find, as I'm certain many before me have been, how very much I wanted to live. In my case I particularly didn't want to die because I wanted to finish my Alice Starmore sweater. The Fair Isle knitting, with its pleasurable two-handed rhythm and constant changes of color, was the most enjoyable I'd ever done. Also, I had things to hide. "If I die," I thought to myself, "my daughter will have to come and clean out my apartment, and when she sees all the yarn stuffed in my kitchen cabinets, she'll think I was insane." I must have had a thousand dollars' worth of yarn stashed in those cabinets. A woman I met last summer who owns a knitting store in St. Paul, Minnesota, told me she had similar fears about her children "wondering just exactly what I was doing with twenty pairs of size six needles."

The next week I was laid off from my job. It hurt, but I had bigger problems to worry about. I felt some peace, however, knowing I was going on vacation to prepare myself for surgery the best way I knew how: with prayer, meditation, nature, fresh air, and knitting.

At Lake Vermilion, some friends took Judy and me on a boat to an island inhabited by bald eagles, more eagles than I had ever seen in one place before. I watched enthralled as they fished and flew, dipped and soared, and regarded us with a jaundiced eye from their various perches around the lake. I felt their presence and the soft wind from their wings as a profound blessing. Then Judy and I drove across northern Minnesota, through forests of evergreens like the ones in my sweater. We drove through the Chippewa National Forest and stopped at

Lake Itasca to see the headwaters of the Mississippi River, which come off the vast lake as a minor trickle among many other creeks. Whenever we stopped for the night I knitted. We traveled across North Dakota and down through South Dakota. I prayed at Bear Butte and again at Pipestone when we returned to Minnesota. In the meantime I was breathing clean air, relaxing, taking Chinese herbs my friend Lydia had given me to strengthen my body before surgery, and working on my sweater. I wanted to live, but I was okay with dying, too, if that was what was going to happen. Inside myself I felt calm and a deep, deep peace.

The surgery went well. I remember being in the operating room, looking around at all the gleaming technology and up at the doctors weirdly covered in their scrubs and saying, "I feel like I'm in a science fiction story."

"This one's a story with a happy ending," said the anesthesiologist, and that was the last thing I heard. According to my doctor, everything had the best possible outcome we could have hoped for. Recovering in the hospital, I had one tense time when my IV started going bad and I needed a doctor to install a new one. I begged her not to put it in my hand, but, against my protests, she did what was most convenient for her. Most of the nurses thought I was making a big fuss over nothing.

Months later I was at Greenwich Yarn in San Francisco. Laurie and Claire, the women who own the store, asked me how I was feeling. "Did you get much knitting done in the hospital?" they wanted to know.

"I couldn't," I said. "I had an IV in my hand." As if on cue, in a single choreographed motion, both of their hands flew up to their faces in horror.

"How could they do that to you?" asked Laurie. "Didn't you tell them you were a knitter?" asked Claire.

Finally I was with people who understood the way I had felt in the hospital. It was fine with me if the doctors took my kidney; I just didn't want them to mess with my hands.

With the surgery over, the cancer successfully gone, my body healing, and my sweater nearing completion, I looked back and realized that I had managed to sail through the whole horrifying episode as calmly as I had primarily because I possessed a secret weapon: my knitting.

Shortly before I had gone into the hospital for surgery, Linda, of the Knitting Basket, had had an accident on her bicycle. She was found on the ground, unconscious, and it took several hours for the doctors to find out what was wrong with her. I dropped by the shop for an update on her condition and learned the news. "She broke her hip," said Betty. "Thank God it's only her hip; she can still knit."

"We're probably the only people in the world who consider a broken hip good news," I said.

What had possessed me in sweltering August heat to dive into a pile of wool that hadn't even been sorted and put away yet? Why was I wild to start a demanding project that very day? And what if I hadn't? The making of that sweater had gotten me through that time as surely as the prayers I had said at sacred places and the skillful hands of my expert surgeon. And when it was all over, I could wear my secret weapon; it no longer had to be concealed.

CHAPTER TWELVE

The Knitting Sutra

FOLLOW THE THREAD, the circle, the web, the pattern that winds through a life. In my middle years I've reached the age of integration and synthesis. I followed a path to the center of my being and stayed for a time, cultivating the garden of my interior self, nourishing the heartwood at my core. When I reemerged, I was traveling a path of my own making. I had become a person—as I once heard it said of the great Sitting Bull—who owns myself.

Sutra, from which comes *suture*, means thread, a connective cord. Our connections to one another are sacred, as all life is sacred, as all of the earth is sacred; the circle that winds around the earth forms the hoop that is also sacred. You don't have to be Native American to know this, only a person of heart. The great unity, the oneness of things, the indivisible interconnectedness of everything that exists in the cosmos is as plain as the nose on your face, if only your eyes are open to see, your ears open to hear.

In Grateful Dead drummer Mickey Hart's book *Drumming at the Edge of Magic*, he talks about a specific moment that occurs when several people drum together, the barely perceptible shift as the drummers "entrain," as he calls it, and their disparate rhythms become one. Native Americans view the drum as the heartbeat of Mother Earth. They bring their babies into the powwow arena, a sacred circle of earth, so that the drumbeat enters their hearts from the very beginning of their lives.

The path I followed to the heart of my being involved rhythm and also a miracle of thread. In knitting one takes a length of thread and, through rhythmic repetitive motions made by clicking two needles together in such a way that they catch the thread, creates interconnecting loops, which eventually grow into a garment to clothe and warm the body. Knitting, like drumming, is a feat of home-grown magic. It is the simplest and most ordinary of activities, yet somehow it mysteriously contains within itself the potential for expanding our conscious awareness.

Buddhists say that enlightenment may be achieved through the repetition of sutra, or prayer. Pattern also is formed by repetition; its beauty deepens and grows each time it is repeated.

When I first saw the Chaucer quote that forms the epigraph to this book, it broke my heart. "The lyf so shorte, the crafte so long to lerne." I thought then that the aim of craft was to become proficient and to spend a lifetime creating beautiful things. It seemed like something was wrong with a plan whereby you took a lifetime to achieve mastery over difficult techniques then died just when you had become really good. I learned while writing this book that the purpose of the craft is not so much to make beautiful things as it is to become beautiful inside while you are making those things.

The finest examples of craftsmanship that come down to us through the ages exalt the human spirit. They belong to us all. They show what we are capable of and what we deserve. Tibetan *thangkas* are pictorial representations of the various Buddhas. Strict requirements must be followed while making them, including maintaining the proper attitude of reverence. Because *thangkas* depict what is most holy in the human spirit, these paintings were made with the finest materials that could be found. Colors were obtained by crushing precious gems into powders: lapis lazuli for the blues, emeralds for the greens, rubies for the reds, and so on. And yet the very finest examples of the *thangka* painters' art manifested not in the fabulous scrolls but inside the painter's self.

That is why the end result, however pleasing to the eye, is ultimately unimportant, and, to show that a work of art may be as impermanent as life itself, Tibetan monks will sometimes ritually destroy the intricate mandalas they painstakingly construct of colored sand.

Pablo Casals, the cellist, once remarked that in music the notes not played are as important as the ones that are played. These are the grace notes, the silent beats of space between audible tones of sound.

Musicians, artists, and craftspeople belong with mystics in the ranks of shamans and visionaries. All reach into the formless void to pull something of substance and beauty out of chaos. What they do may manifest on the material plane, but their goals reach beyond materialism to a representation of spirit itself. Picasso claimed that he was able to maintain the stamina he needed for painting well into his eighties because when he entered his studio he left his body at the door. There is an ecstasy in the act of creation that matches the intensity of religious rapture; both partake of divinity and are gifts granted by the Great Creative Spirit.

Other people may have other gifts, such as healing the sick, foretelling the future, or understanding the language of animals, birds, and plants. I think I would like to cultivate a talent for the latter. I can foresee a happy old age for myself, conversing with birds in the trees. Maybe that will come later in my life; I certainly hope so. I would definitely consider that a worthwhile form of enlightenment. One of the best things about having Hayat for a friend was that I could watch her, at ninety-four, and think to myself, "I'd like to grow up to be just like her."

Oren Lyons, the faithkeeper of the Onondaga tribe, part of the Iroquois confederacy that contributed the model of democratic government adopted in the Declaration of Independence, says that when making major decisions, his tribe does things "for the seventh generation yet unborn." This perspective allows one to look further into the future and arrange for the preservation of resources rather than stripping the land for short-term gain and letting future generations worry about themselves.

It is a truism of spiritual studies that you cannot ask for knowledge to be given you for your own benefit. You receive spiritual knowledge only as a sacred trust; you vow to be a channel and transmit whatever you learn for the benefit of all sentient beings. I've heard it said that in the Sufi schools you cannot advance to the next level of attainment until you have trained someone else to take your place in the level you are leaving.

For myself, I am no great scholar. I have allowed my studies in many traditions to lapse. I'm a nonobservant Jew, an Arican who doesn't do trainings, a woefully negligent Sufi. I haven't taken opportunities that were offered to me to delve further into the teachings of Native American ways. I maintained, whether right or wrong, a stubborn insistence on doing only what appealed to me at the time, according to the dictates of my own heart. I trusted no outside authority, although I had the great good fortune of encountering teachers who were the equal of anyone on the planet. If what I chose is dangerous or the height of lunacy, I take full responsibility; the arrogance and lunacy are entirely my own.

I would never presume to tell someone else that knitting is a path to enlightenment or even a meditation in and of itself. Knitting is a meditative activity and can form a kind of practice. But then, almost anything can be a spiritual practice. Writing can become your daily practice or walking or surfing or growing the finest watermelons on God's green earth. I believe there are places you can reach only with a spiritual guide. Much of what I know and experienced I would not have been able to accomplish on my own. But all of it brought me to a point where I had to, as Huck so memorably said, "light out for the territory ahead." Alone, with no one to guide me; I had to find my own way through the woods.

Shortly after I had broken my arm, my friends Karen and Charley Osborne took me camping to their place in Big Creek, in the wilds of woolly Big Sur. A house carved in the Haida style, after one of the Northwest coastal tribes that specialized in monumental totem poles, stands on their property. The animals and spirit beings carved from the weathered wood possess an unmistakable power, which the setting only enhances. In Big Sur the immanence of spirit in the land is nothing more or less than incontrovertible fact. I bathed my arm in the icy waters of the fast-running river and tried to connect with the resident spirits to ask for aid in my healing.

At the time I was just at the beginning of the journey described in this book. I hadn't yet gone to Arizona with Jimmy or met Hayat or started to knit. I had only recently begun doing regular weekly *zikrs*. My writing was on hold, my health was in crisis, and I didn't have a clue what I was supposed to be doing in Arica. Karen and I had long talks, as we have continued to do throughout our friendship, about spiritual life in general and our relationships to our various teachers specifically.

"I don't know, Sue," she said to me one day as we trudged through fallen leaves toward the rickety wooden bridge across the creek, "I have a feeling something is about to happen to you, but I don't know what it is. It's like you're gathering power around you, attracting these interesting people into your life, shaking things up for a reason. I'd like to check back with you in about five years and see how it all came out."

A few weeks ago Karen came into the Knitting Basket on a day I happened to be sitting there with Linda. "I feel like I'm entering the inner sanctum of the saints," she said. Of course she was joking, and all of us laughed, but it occurred to me that I've learned as much from Linda over the years as I have from my other spiritual teachers. I am not her equal as a knitter and may never be, but I'm considerably better than I was technically and am utterly transformed in the way I view the craft.

I now teach classes in knitting for beginners. What I have to give as a teacher is not so much an ability to transmit the basics of technique, though I can do that perfectly well, as a desire to kindle the spark of inspiration in my students by sharing my own love of the craft with them. Ultimately it is only that love that will motivate them to continue knitting, driving them forward through awkwardness and frustration, through the heartache of failed projects and the smug exhilaration of successful ones, toward the real reward that lies within themselves.

The purpose of meditation is to quiet the mind so that it can sink down into contemplation of its true nature. You cannot stop your mind by an act of will any more than you can stop the beating of your own heart. Some cultures describe mind as a drunken monkey, reeling from place to place with no rhyme or reason. Like meditation, knitting calms the monkey down. The purpose of *zikr*, as described by Sheikh Taner, is to annihilate the false self, the ego self, so that the real self, the inner being, has a chance to shine through. I believe that in the quiet, repetitive, hypnotic rhythms of creating craft, the inner being may emerge in all its quiet beauty. The very rhythms of the knitting needles can become as incantatory as a drumbeat or a Gregorian chant.

For years my sister Lorraine belonged to the Integral Yoga Institute, Swami Satchidananda's ashram. I always liked their motto: "Paths are many; truth is one." Follow whatever thread you find till you come to the place that you're seeking.

There is a German proverb that goes, "Begin to weave and God will give the thread."

CHAPTER THIRTEEN

The Zen of Nonattachment

LETTING GO IS THE LESSON. Letting go is always the lesson. Have you ever noticed how much of our agony is all tied up with craving and loss?

The worst has happened. I can't knit anymore. Earlier in my life I knitted in binges, and the binges were separated from one another by long stretches of nonknitting time, sometimes years. Since I broke my arm, I've been knitting steadily, without ceasing, for over five years. In that span of time I've learned more about knitting than I had in the whole previous thirty years, and about living, too.

But knitting steadily and as much as I did, I never gave my hands a chance to rest and recover. Nothing could be more conducive to repetitive stress injury than the small, delicate motions of knitting. Pinch your thumb and index finger into a circle and move it back and forth with a slight flick of your wrist. Add a small measure of obsession-compulsion. Voilà! Instant carpal tunnel syndrome.

Well, maybe just tendonitis. Or a touch of arthritis. Pain. Stiffness. Numbness. Scary stuff. My friend Norman Kennedy worked as the master weaver at Colonial Williamsburg for years, until carpal tunnel syndrome put an end to his career. He can knit, but he has to be vigilant about not overdoing it. Otherwise his hands get so bad that he can't twist a lid off a jar or turn a doorknob. I make a living at my computer. I can't afford to have my hands quit on me.

My acupuncturist puts needles in my wrists. "Don't knit for a week," he tells me. Is this man insane? Maybe *he's* not, but *I* certainly am. Nevertheless, I put down my knitting needles. During meetings I'm so nervous and fidgety I can hardly sit still in my seat. When I awake in the morning, a time I usually knit and reflect, I wander around at a dead loss. My peace of mind is completely shattered, serenity totally gone.

I go to the Knitting Basket to complain. Linda also has been having problems with her wrists. "Oh, dear," Sheila says to me. "But you *need* your knitting. This is not a hobby; it's therapy, especially for the likes of you."

At the end of the week I start knitting again, trying to make up for lost time, and within a day or two my wrists are as bad as they were before the treatment. Linda says one problem is that we're both making Alice Starmore sweaters on tiny needles, concentrating hard every minute.

By now I'm making my third Fair Isle, a long-sleeved pullover in corals and blues. Of course I'm dying to see what it looks like; there's simply no way I'm going to put it aside for a few months. Besides, I've noticed that when I knit with big needles and bulkier yarn, the pain just goes into my elbows. If I knit in plain stockinette, without any color or pattern changes, the repetitive motion stress is more severe. And so on.

A sane person would probably give it a rest. But I go to my chiropractor, the fabulous Dr. Walton, wizard of vertebrae, magician of lower backs. He adjusts my neck, my upper back, my shoulder, my elbow, all the places the tendon runs through. He gets things moving that have been frozen in place since the ice age. He tweaks my hands, my fingers, my wrists. Then he lowers the boom. "Put yourself on the injured list," he says. "No knitting for two weeks."

Quitting knitting is a lot like quitting smoking. The first few days are the roughest. Sometimes I can't remember that I've quit; I'm only vaguely aware of something missing, not quite conscious what it is. My fingers feel unaccountably lonely. I long for the comforting rhythms and colors of the Alice Starmore sweater. I wonder if I'll ever get back to it. One factor driving my compulsive rush to the bitter end is the historical memory of all the projects I put aside and never picked up again. My old habit of abandoning my sweaters midway through the second sleeve now haunts me. Even now, too many solitary backs of abandoned sweaters languish in my kitchen cabinets, along with unworked surpluses of yarn.

It takes a long time for my hands to feel better. Two weeks stretches into four. Even after four I can knit for only a little while before pain starts shooting up my arm. It reminds me of when I was in college and all I liked to do was play my guitar. My grandmother, Mama Yetta, had then recently been forced to stop crocheting because arthritis bothered her hands, and I remember worrying that I would get arthritis in my hands and not be able to play guitar.

It's odd, too, because I've really branched out in my knitting. I used to say that I would knit only for myself. Partly this was because I never knew when I might grow tired of a project and put it aside, sometimes forever; partly it was because I might spoil it with a ghastly mistake. I couldn't promise that the sweater would come out looking like the pattern or be the size that I set out to make. I could take those risks for myself but not for someone else.

But as I've gotten better, I can knit for others as easily as I can for myself. I often sell sweaters I've completed, because the volume of my knitting is more than I could possibly use for myself. Two years ago I knitted my daughter her first sweater since baby days. She came along to the yarn shop with me and picked out both the yarn and the style, which turned out a terrific success. I've also knitted things that people requested, although even several years ago I would have said that I couldn't possibly knit under those conditions.

Somehow the more my knitting has improved, and the better the quality of product I turn out, the easier it's become for me to let go of what I knit, to detach from it, to view the finished article not as the be-all and end-all of my activity but as a means to an end, the end being what happened to me while I knitted it. I have a lot more security that I will actually finish what I start, that I'll pay attention to the crafting and make it as well as I can, that I'll advance my level of skill, and that it will be made to fit and to last. My rewards are no longer the finished garments but the invisible lessons I garnered while making them. I've become a process- rather than a product-oriented knitter; I enjoy the activity for its own sake, which is probably a bit of spiritual advancement, as these things go.

For the time being, though, I've expanded as far as I could, and now I'm having to pull back a bit, contract again; I'm forced to think long and hard about what I'm going to make in the short bursts of knitting time my hands will allow me.

The Buddha said that all suffering comes from our desires. Some spiritual paths require that you let go of worldly ambitions, renounce material security, learn to reach without grasping, hold without strangling, practice nonattachment, detach with love. "Let go and let God," the saying goes.

Aaaargh!

My friend John Hosford, who studied to be a blacksmith and practiced the trade until carpal tunnel syndrome set in, tells me that the Japanese believe each trade holds within it the tools needed for achieving enlightenment. In other words, in Japan a tofu maker can become enlightened as easily as a martial artist. This jibes with a favorite Zen saying of mine: "How you do anything is how you do everything."

For the past five years I've been consciously knitting. I set out to achieve proficiency and mastery, both of which I now have. So what do I do with these qualities now, when I can no longer knit?

Simple: I knit without knitting. I take all the lessons I've learned while knitting and apply them to the rest of my life. I sit still. I take time for quiet reflection. I center myself and direct my attention to what's in front of me. I continue to let my spirit loose in the fertile fields of creativity, imagining colors, textures, and shapes in various combinations, though I may not be able to realize these visions materially. Whatever I'm doing, I keep going through the difficult parts, even when I want to give up. When I feel discomfort, I don't automatically run or seek to change my feelings. I focus on the journey rather than the goal. Buddhist teacher Sylvia Boorstein says that mindfulness "is the aware, balanced acceptance of present experience." I try to accept whatever is going on in my life, including the fact that for the time being, I cannot knit.

Nevertheless, I've reached some new level with my knitting. While paying attention to the tiniest of details, without knowing it was happening, I came to embody the principles, the abstracts, the fundamental structures, the inner part of the craft, its essence and spirit. Now knitting is mine whether I do it or not.

Letting go seems to be one of those concepts that lends itself to understanding mainly through paradox. The twelve-step programs have a saying that goes, "You have to give it away to keep it." In all my creative efforts, whether they involve words or fiber, there's always one constant. Nothing I make ever lives up to the initial vision I had for it; reality always falls short of my dreams. In a way that's what keeps me going; if I were to realize all my visions, what would be the point of doing more? I've heard it said that no poem is ever finished; it's simply abandoned. I've never made a sweater that I couldn't, the minute it was completed, do over and get better the second time. But there comes a point where you have to let go. Set it free, whatever it is; release it to the universe with love. Besides, the older you get, the less time you have available for running the world and making sure everything comes out right.

Once at a party in New York, Oscar Ichazo, who founded the Arica school, told a group of his students a story about the young tiger and the old tiger. The young tiger was strong and full of energy. He ran around all day stalking and chasing prey; sometimes he got a meal; sometimes the meal ran away. The old tiger, meanwhile, just lay in the grass in the shade all day and slept. He was old; he was tired; he needed his rest. At the end of the day he woke up, stretched, and ambled out to the edge of the bush, just in time to see his meal on wheels approaching. The old tiger lifted up his paw, brought it down on the prey, and whap! there was dinner. Then he rolled over and went back to sleep.

I don't know how or when it happened, but I've become the old tiger. I may not be able to do much, but I know just what to do. There's economy and mastery in my movements. I didn't plan it, didn't foresee it, couldn't imagine from the vantage point of youth what earthly good could possibly come of aging, but now that it's here, I've welcomed it in. What is, is. I accept it with grace.

Epilogue:
Taking Flight

WINGS ARE NOT ENOUGH, it seems. We must also grow roots to hold us fast to earth. I am reminded of a story I read in a book about Alaska, *Inside Passage,* by Michael Modzelewski. Bald eagles capture salmon with their talons but can lift them into the air only if the fish weigh less than ten pounds or so. Sometimes, when the salmon outweighs what the bird can carry and the eagle's talons are sunk too deeply in the fish's flesh to be withdrawn, the salmon may drag the bird underwater and swim with the eagle on its back until it drowns.

Fishermen in Alaska have been known to catch salmon whose heads are crowned with eagle talons.

The moral of the story? Even an eagle has to lift off from solid ground.

Knitting grounds me in the realness of the physical world. The feel of the yarn in my fingers, the steady growth of the fabric, the soothing click of the needles, the attention required to stay on course all help to hold me close to terra firma. Though mind and spirit travel in the cosmos, beyond the moon and stars, my body stays rooted in comforting solidity. I've come to appreciate solidity in these last few years, to value strength, an unshakable core.

Some days I luxuriate in solitude like a cat basking in the sun. I've fallen in love with the whole of creation, the redwood trees, the fingers of fog, raptors tracing circles in the sky. I'm living a life that I always imagined but never knew how to find.

Lately I've been thinking back to the time I lived in New York, during the seventies and early eighties. I remember the knitting I wanted to do then, the fantasies I had for what I would make. For years I carried around a pattern my friend Mary Peacock had brought me back from England, for a Fair Isle pullover. I bought the yarn but never made the sweater because I couldn't figure out how to do it. When designing my projects I always wanted to take a neckline from here, a sleeve from there, the body from still another pattern, but I did not yet possess the skills to realize my visions. Today I knit the way I always wanted to. I possess a casual mastery; I know what to do to alter a shape, whip up a quick alteration, change a pattern to suit my whims in midstream, as it were. There are plenty of knitters more proficient than I, but I'm content now because I have the skills that I always desired.

Sometimes I wonder how I managed to stay with knitting long enough to get here. I can read myself dry or exhaust any number of entertainments and obsessions within a matter of weeks or months. But just when I think I've exhausted knitting, it suddenly falls off into deeper waters, like one of those abrupt drops near the edges of the oceans, and I'm off exploring new territory again. I can only describe it as similar to a love affair that renews and regenerates itself each time you think it's over. The craft of knitting has been one of the great enduring loves of my life.

Knitting rooted itself in my heart and helped my heart sprout wings.

Hayat once told me that a giant dark wing had covered the windows of her house one day. I have felt the presence of spirits and the wind from wild birds' wings, yet if anyone had asked me what I'd been doing, I would have answered, "Nothing much. Just knitting."

While I was knitting the maelstrom swirled around me, bringing me everything that was meant to be mine. In *zikr* the heart flies to the Beloved on wings. Our minds, too, have wings, on which soar feelings, thoughts, and fantasies, a free fall through possibilities, an exhilaration in the thrill of creation and the joy of being alive.

I didn't have to be airborne, just focused within myself.

Whoosh!

What is flight but a displacement of air?

It all comes down to one of those pesky paradoxes.

Sitting still, I had learned how to fly.

Acknowledgments

THANKS TO RUHAMA VELTFORT for giving me the idea for this book; Tom Grady for greeting it warmly; my agents, David Black and Susan Raihofer, for doing their job so well; Mary Peacock for editorial wisdom and expertise; and my Harper San Francisco editors, Caroline Pincus and Mimi Kusch, for care and concern, as usual, above and beyond the call of professional duty.

I had the benefit of deep, searching conversations on the subject, at times when my enthusiasm flagged and needed renewing, with Rhoda Creamer, Judith Stronach,

Norman Kennedy, Jessica Jones, John Hosford, and David Getz.

Barbara and Michael Kossen, Natalie Mucyn and Herb Solomon, Rick Kahn, Laureen Bethards, Terry LaRue, Carolyn Baugh, Lyle Poncher, Paddy Berne, Louisa Jaskulski, Jeanne Gloe, Joel Schmukler, Dr. Ellen Gunther, Judy Coburn, Marilyn Rinzler, Jan McNeil, Lydia García, Anne Pierce, and Dr. Charles Turzan, among others too numerous to mention, were especially kind to me during events described in this book.

Special thanks to Betty Cooper, Guy Manybeads, and "Jimmy Woodbine" for everything they taught me. *Aho! Mitakuye Oyasin.*

Various issues of *Vogue Knitting* and *Knitter's Magazine* proved helpful. The book *No Idle Hands: The Social History of American Knitting,* by Anne L. MacDonald, was my source for information that the American Red Cross evolved from Civil War knitting circles. My thanks to Johnny Rotten for locating the Chaucer quote in *The Canterbury Tales.*

Round up the usual suspects! My friends, Linda ("Lou") Vestal, Victor and the Ratto family, Kathy Ogle, Polly Frizzell, Karen Osborne, Paule and Emmett Marx, Genie and Duncan McNaughton, Steve and Claudia Stroud, the Ishi Study Group, the Thursday night bridge regulars, Daniel Dale, Arthur Littlebear, Alan Ledford,

Terry Mercherson, Judy Moore, Sue Kearney, Ani Chamichian, Caroline Herter, Kate Coleman, Suzy Nelson, Lee Ann Sandefer, and Anne Weills all served as cheerleaders for various stages of the project.

My beloved family, the Gordons and Wolffs, and daughter, Shuna Lydon, were with me in spirit and heart through the writing of this book.

Thanks to the Knitting Basket for giving me a home away from home and to computer wizard Camilo Wilson for tech support.

I wish to acknowledge my teacher, Oscar Ichazo, and the Arica School. I owe a debt of gratitude to Sheikh Taner Vargonen and the late Hayat Stadlinger for their generous gift of heart. Always I value the support of my recovering brothers and sisters in the East Bay area.

A bow to all the craftspeople, past, present, and future, who spread beauty through the world with the patient and skillful work of their hands.

Ēpūpūkahi. We are one.